*William Studwell, MSLS*

# The Christmas Carol Reader

*Pre-publication
REVIEWS,
COMMENTARIES,
EVALUATIONS . . .*

"**C**hristmas carols are so thoroughly woven into our lives that it is all too easy to view them as devoid of any authentic historical implications; fictions and misconceptions about popular carols abound, and are often repeated without challenge. William Studwell's *The Christmas Carol Reader* changes this for the better. In these concise and witty essays, Studwell dispels the myths that surround so many carols and explains their true, and far more fascinating, origins. Libraries everywhere will find this useful for answering the perennial queries about Christmas songs; general readers will enjoy browsing through its many surprises."

**H. Stephen Wright, MMus, MLS**
*Associate Professor/Music Librarian,
Northern Illinois University*

From 'O Come, O Come Emmanuel' to 'White Christmas,' from 'Silent Night' to 'Jingle Bells,' and from 'Lo, How a Rose' to 'Rudolph the Red Nosed Reindeer,' Studwell runs the gamut with fascinating comments on the persons, places, situations, and events that shaped the most significant cultural choral contributions in our currently complex civilization."

**Dr. Leonard W. Van Camp**
*Director of Choral Activities,*
*Southern Illinois University*
*at Edwardsville*

"**H** ow can a 'reference book' be so much fun to read? Or how can such a charming, witty, and enjoyable layperson's book be so scholarly? William Studwell's delightful *The Christmas Carol Reader* is filled with interesting information about a wide range of Christmas songs that, in his generous definition, are 'carols.' He does not quote sources for his findings, for he is himself an unimpeachable source for anything you might care to know about a wide range of yuletide musical gems, spanning centuries and encompassing the globe.

Both the words and music receive thoughtful, thorough, and scholarly examination–but the paragraphs that result from Studwell's conclusions are as pithy and pungent as they are entertaining and enlightening. Every library in the English-speaking world should own this book–as should choral directors, singers, pastors, teachers, amateur musicologists, and average people who simply love Christmas music.

"**T** he Christmas Carol Reader by William Studwell is one of those books librarians love to have around for reference. In one volume, 140 essays detail the origins and history of 140 carols. I recommend this book for school, public, and academic libraries."

**Linda Hartig, PhD**
*Music Librarian,*
*University of Wisconsin,*
*Milwaukee*

"**T**radition has decreed that the merriment and joy of the Christmas season shall at least equal, if not predominate over, the serious awesomeness of the Christmas Event. Here is a book full of joy, which embodies its author's lighthearted approach to the study of the songs of Christmas. It is a treasury of information. Those who read it straight through, or who use it to enhance the understanding of their choirs' renditions, or who precede group carol-singing with interesting comments gleaned from its pages, will hardly realize they are educating or being educated.

The scope of *The Christmas Carol Reader* sweeps from the fourth century, when the poetry of 'Savior of the Nations, Come' was first heard, through the twentieth century's creation of a large body of popular songs such as 'A Holly Jolly Christmas' and 'White Christmas.' Great names in music glitter like jewels through the pages.

William Studwell allows us to sense the ambiance of the cultural cocoon in which a carol was born. This is a book for reading or for reference."

**Dorothy E. Jones**
*Reference Librarian,*
*Northern Illinois University Libraries*

"**W**illiam Studwell's *The Christmas Carol Reader* is an excellent history of this ubiquitous yet little known area of our cultural history. Though Christmas carols are among the most familiar kinds of music, their origins and histories are almost unknown. Mr. Studwell's book sheds a bright light on this corner of our Western heritage (not to mention our popular culture). Mr. Studwell ranges from the mists of medieval times to post-World War II songs, and from the sacred to the secular. Indeed, the Christmas carol's longevity and variety astonish the reader of this book.

*The Christmas Carol Reader* is a welcome addition to the literature on carols and also explores a neglected aspect of popular culture. The book is highly recommended."

**Bruce R. Schueneman, MLS, MS**
*Coordinator of Technical Services,*
*Texas A&M University,*
*Kingsville*

"William Studwell's *The Christmas Carol Reader* is in essence a reference work. But do not let its substance scare you off. This book reads like few other reference works as Studwell takes what is so very familiar and uncovers its meaning and usage over the ages. Cleverly arranged, it ranges over carols that treat Christmas as a holy day, and those that discuss Christmas as a holiday—one might say the sacred and the secular.

The carols within have both reflected and molded culture and theology. By compiling and commenting on the songs that the church and society have sung over the past ages, Studwell penetrates the way people have understood the Christian message of Christmas both in sacred and secular terms, and gives us clues as to how we view this event in the present. Should your favorite carol be missing from the table of contents, don't worry. If it is at all important, Studwell will mention it somewhere in the text. This book furnishes a broad yet comprehensive view of the carols that continue to shape current celebrations of Christmas and is a must read for those interested in theology and culture. Studwell is, as always, exciting and illuminating."

**Lawrence R. Rast, Jr., STM, MDiv**
*PhD Candidate,*
*Vanderbilt University,*
*Nashville, Tennessee*

Harrington Park Press
An Imprint of The Haworth Press, Inc.

## NOTES FOR PROFESSIONAL LIBRARIANS AND LIBRARY USERS

This is an original book title published by Harrington Park Press, an imprint of The Haworth Press, Inc. Unless otherwise noted in specific chapters with attribution, materials in this book have not been previously published elsewhere in any format or language.

## CONSERVATION AND PRESERVATION NOTES

All books published by The Haworth Press, Inc. and its imprints are printed on certified ph neutral, acid free book grade paper. This paper meets the minimum requirements of American National Standard for Information Sciences–Permanence of Paper for Printed Material, ANSI Z39.48-1984.

# The Christmas Carol Reader

# *HAWORTH* Popular Culture
## Frank W. Hoffmann, PhD and William G. Bailey, MA
### Senior Editors

New, Recent, and Forthcoming Titles:

*Arts & Entertainment Fads* by Frank W. Hoffmann and William G. Bailey

*Sports & Recreation Fads* by Frank W. Hoffmann and William G. Bailey

*Mind & Society Fads* by Frank W. Hoffmann and William G. Bailey

*Fashion & Merchandising Fads* by Frank W. Hoffmann and William G. Bailey

*Chocolate Fads, Folklore, and Fantasies: 1000+ Chunks of Chocolate Information* by Linda K. Fuller

*The Popular Song Reader: A Sampler of Well-Known Twentieth Century Songs* by William Studwell

*Rock Music in American Popular Culture: Rock 'n' Roll Resources* by B. Lee Cooper and Wayne S. Haney

*Great Awakenings: Popular Religion and Popular Culture* by Marshall W. Fishwick

*The Christmas Carol Reader* by William Studwell

# The Christmas Carol Reader

William Studwell, MSLS

Harrington Park Press
An Imprint of The Haworth Press, Inc.
New York • London

Published by

Harrington Park Press, an imprint of The Haworth Press, Inc., 10 Alice Street, Binghamton, NY 13904-1580

**Library of Congress Cataloging-in-Publication Data**

Studwell, William E. (William Emmett), 1936-
 The Christmas carol reader / William Studwell.
  p.   cm.
 Includes index.
 ISBN 1-56023-872-0 (pbk. : alk. paper)
 1. Carols–History and criticism.
ML2880.S78 1995
782.28'1723'09–dc20                                                      95-17627
                                                                           CIP
                                                                           MN

# CONTENTS

# ABOUT THE AUTHOR

**William E. Studwell, MSLS,** is Professor, University Libraries, at Northern Illinois University in DeKalb. He is the author of seven books on music including reference books on popular songs, Christmas carols, ballet, and opera, as well as three books on cataloging. He has also authored about 200 articles in library science and music and has made more than 150 radio, television, and print appearances in national, regional, and local media. Mr. Studwell is the editor of *Music Reference Services Quarterly.*

# Introduction

It may be presumptuous to compare this volume to the fabled star of Bethlehem. Yet like that biblical astronomical body, the intent of this collection of 140 essays is to enlighten and to guide. Gathered herein is a composite picture of the world's most important and famous carols plus an ample supply of lesser-known Christmas songs which for one reason or another add to the fulfillment of the Christmas music scene. All of the carols are presented in their chronological and cultural contexts, which will, I hope, help to understand and appreciate the songs, and in an unabashedly nonobjective and sometimes unconventional manner, which will, I further hope, help to sustain the lively spirit of the season.

This book can be approached in three different ways. On long winter nights, the reader can treat it as a series of fact-based commentaries to be continuously read. For shorter periods between holiday activities, one of the 19 topical sections can be perused or an individual essay can be selected. To aid in the location of a particular carol, the reader can consult the title index at the back.

The carols in each topical section are not completely distinct from the ones in other groupings, since many carols could easily be placed in multiple categories. The choice was admittedly personal and subjective, but at the same time consciously designed to batch together songs with some degree of shared holiday theme. Just as it is often difficult to categorize individual carols, it has been historically difficult to define what a Christmas carol might actually be. If the realities of holiday music are fully viewed, perhaps the best and certainly the most convenient description of a carol is any song used to celebrate any aspect of the colorful spectrum of the Christmas period. Advent, Epiphany, the New Year, and to some extent the winter season are all included in the delightful and culturally significant body of sacred and secular music which greatly enhances the end of each calendar year.

One of the principal causes of confusion about the definition of the Christmas carol is the long, somewhat elusive, and generally obscure historical trail left by the 16 centuries of wanderings by this seasonal music phenomenon. Because the carol has been usually treated as a minor genre, most often far removed from the mainstream of Western artistic activity, the carol has not received a great deal of attention from those persons chronicling our past. Yet enough of a historical Christmas music package can be assembled using slender ribbons of trends and shiny bits of paper facts gleaned from the centuries of holiday celebration.

The earliest known carol of consequence was "Veni, Redemptor gentium" ("Savior of the Nations, Come"), a Latin hymn probably written by St. Ambrose in the late fourth century. For the next 1,000 years, there were relatively few Christmas songs written, and mainly in Latin or Greek. Generally, these songs are obscure today, but there are some notable exceptions. For example, in the twelfth century, both the lyrics and melody for the Latin carol "Veni, Emmanuel" ("O Come, O Come, Emmanuel") may have been created. If so, that song would be the oldest well-known carol. However, the medieval dating of the two components of "Veni, Emmanuel" is definitely suspect, and in any case the words and music were not brought together as a unit until the middle of the nineteenth century. If that song is not the oldest famous carol, then the next candidate for that honor is the vigorous thirteenth-century folk piece from Provence in Southern France, "La marche des rois" ("The March of the Kings").

With the appearance of "La marche des rois" and some other carols of the thirteenth and fourteenth centuries such as "W zlobie lezy" ("Jesus Holy, Born So Lowly") from Poland and "In dulci jubilo," a combination Latin/vernacular song from Germany, a trend began in carols. Songs in the everyday language of the people began to appear, and in a few centuries mostly replaced the language of the Church as the medium for composition of carols. Not coincidentally, another major development in the history of Christmas music appeared at about the same time. Around 1400 in England, and somewhat earlier on the continent, the carol evolved as a popular dance form in reaction to the strictness of the Middle Ages.

(The word "carol" is probably a derivative of the Greek word "choros," meaning "dance.")

These new developments ended a 1,000-year span of comparative stagnation and heralded the dawn of the golden age of the carol. Fully compatible with the creative spirit, increased secularism, and humanism of the late medieval period and the Renaissance, the carol blossomed in the fifteenth and sixteenth centuries. In the fifteenth century came songs such as "I Saw Three Ships," "Coventry Carol," and "The Boar's Head Carol" from England, plus "Es ist ein Ros' entsprungen" ("Lo, How a Rose E'er Blooming") from Germany. In the even greater sixteenth century (arguably the finest epoch of the carol), the British classics "Deck the Halls with Boughs of Holly," "The First Nowell," and "God Rest You Merry, Gentlemen" were most likely created, with the German carol "O Tannenbaum" ("O Christmas Tree") also possibly from that time.

The seventeenth and eighteenth centuries were much less productive for the carol, in large part due to the overall more conservative atmosphere then prevalent. For example, the secular observance of Christmas was actually banned for several years, beginning in 1644, by the English Puritans. However, some fine carols were created in this two-century period of semi-dormancy, including "Wassail Song," "The Twelve Days of Christmas," and "The Holly and the Ivy" from England, plus "Adeste fideles" ("O Come All Ye Faithful") and "Les anges dans nos campagnes" ("Angels We Have Heard on High") from France.

A resurgence of interest in the carol came in the nineteenth century, revitalized in part by such celebrated holiday writings as Clement Moore's 1822 "'Twas the Night before Christmas" and Charles Dickens' 1843 *A Christmas Carol.* "Stille Nacht, heilige Nacht" ("Silent Night") from Austria, "Cantique de Noël" ("O Holy Night") from France, plus "It Came upon the Midnight Clear," "We Three Kings of Orient Are," "O Little Town of Bethlehem," and "Jingle Bells" from the United States were among songs written in that active century. Add to the composition of carols a large amount of carol collecting, translating, arranging, etc., done during the 1800s, and the nineteenth century becomes a most important era for Christmas music.

The twentieth century witnessed yet another swing in the overall pattern of the carol. Increasingly, secular themes began to dominate over sacred ones, particularly in the United States. This trend has become especially evident after World War II in America, for successful U.S. religious carols after that date have been very rare. Although the many good secular Christmas songs produced in recent decades are an asset to the celebration of the holiday, it is hoped that the composition of fine religious carols has not become a lost art.

This brief overview of the history of the carol suggests that despite being generally simple as individual entities, carols as a group are quite multifaceted and complex. Carols have taken many forms, have come from a number of different cultures, and have been created in varying time environments. The only thing that all these songs have in common is their distinct tendency to be performed around Christmastime, year after year after year, by diverse segments of society. Continuity and cultural pervasiveness allow the "lowly" carol to cast a perhaps surprising amount of influence on Western civilization. It demonstrates that something common and for the average person can be a significant positive force in our lives and also bring a great deal of enjoyment into our existence.

# PART I:
# CHRISTMAS AS A HOLY DAY

# THE BIRTH OF JESUS

## Away in a Manger

Some well-chosen and strategically placed words can create misinformation that remains in the popular imagination for many years. This was the situation when the lyrics and melody for "Away in a Manger" were first published in 1887. Because the song was printed with the heading "Luther's Cradle Hymn (Composed by Martin Luther for his children, and still sung by German mothers to their little ones)," it was widely believed that the great historical figure was its author. After all, Luther (1483-1546) did compose several hymns, notably "A Mighty Fortress Is Our God" (1527 or 1528) and the carol "From Heaven Above to Earth I Come" (1534-1539).

It took nearly 60 years to disprove this modern myth. Research published in 1945 clearly demonstrated that Luther was not at all responsible for either words or music. The genesis of the myth was perhaps an 1872 book, *Luther at Home*, by T. B. Stork. At the time Lutherans were strongly attracted to a series of sentimental illustrations about Luther's family life. Stork made the statement that "Luther's carol for Christmas, written for his own child Hans, is still sung." Quite possibly Stork was referring to Luther's carol "From Heaven Above" which had received its best-known translation only a few years before, in 1855. But Stork did not specifically name the carol he alluded to, thus creating the potential for misunderstanding.

In 1885, another troublesome element was inserted into this vacuum of underinformation and sentimentality. In that year two anonymous verses entitled "Away in a Manger" appeared in a collection of Lutheran hymns published in Philadelphia. No authorship for these verses has ever been ascertained, except for the possibility of association with the German Lutheran community of Pennsylvania. (A third verse, added before 1892, is also anonymous.) Two years after the publication of the enigmatic verses, the lyrics were again issued, this time in Cincinnati, Ohio, and this time with a musical setting and the very misleading attribution to Martin Luther. The editor of the infamous 1887 collection, American James Ramsey Murray (1841-1905), was almost surely the composer of the gentle melody. But due to the environment of misinformation his authorship was not determined until much later, in spite of the notation "Music by J. R. M." indicated when the lullaby was next published in 1888. One can only conjecture about Murray's motivation for the misrepresentation of the song as Luther's. Perhaps he was caught up in the Luther sentimentality fad and really thought that the lyrics were by Luther. Or perhaps he decided to take advantage of the prevailing mood and to use the name of Luther to draw attention to his melody. Either way, the effect was to evoke immediate interest in the carol.

Further elements of confusion were added over the years by the incorrect attribution of the tune to a possibly imaginary personage named "Carl Mueller" and by the publication of the lyrics with a large number of variant tunes. Of the abundant substitute melodies, the most used are a tune by Jonathan E. Spilman (1812-1896) created for the song "Flow Gently, Sweet Afton" and a melody by William James Kirkpatrick (1838-1921) which is commonly sung in Great Britain. Despite the knowledge that Luther and Mueller are in no way associated with the writing of the carol, the myth continues. Some collections in the 1980s still indicate that Luther and/or Mueller are the creators of "Away in a Manger." The same type of situation, almost unbelievably, also applies to two other great Christmas songs, "Joy to the World!" and "O Come All Ye Faithful." Perhaps our later twentieth-century society is not as knowledgeable and sophisticated as we would like to think.

# The Babe

Mexico has two main cultural heritages. The oldest is the rich Indian tradition of the Aztecs, Mayas, Mixtecs, and others, which dates back an unknown number of centuries. The more recent is the dominant Spanish culture which was introduced into Mexico with the conquests of Hernán Cortés and his soldiers beginning in 1519. Due largely to this blend of civilizations, the folk music of Mexico, though having definite affiliations with the arts of Spain, has a style which is distinct from that of the "mother country."

As early as the seventeenth century, baroque-style Christmas music appeared in Mexico. This music, however, was strongly influenced by Spain. It was not until possibly the eighteenth century that New World-style folk carols came onto the Mexican scene. All of the notable Mexican folk Christmas songs were probably created during that century or the nineteenth century. The best known of these carols is perhaps "El rorro," most typically translated as "The Babe," but with variant titles such as "Rocking the Child," "The Rocking of the Child," and "O, Ru-Ru-Ru, My Little Jesus." This lullaby is traditionally sung on Christmas Eve as the climax of a nine-night "Posadas" ceremony reenacting Mary and Joseph's search for lodging.

"The Babe" is one of the few Latin American carols that is known in the United States. "El Mino Jesus" ("The Child Jesus") from Puerto Rico and "Vamos pastoricitos" ("Let Us Go, O Shepherds") from Colombia are others that are also moderately used north of the Rio Grande. But no Latin American carol is particularly familiar to United States audiences, a condition which is a bit surprising considering the wealth of Latin American music known to norteamericanos.

# The Birthday of a King

If the typical American was asked to name a birthday song, the response would almost surely be "Happy Birthday to You." Such an answer would be nearly automatic, for the simple American children's song from the late nineteenth century (1893) is arguably the most sung piece of music in the United States. But if the first question were followed up by a second request to name still another birthday song, the chances are that the reply would not be as readily given. Yet when one really thinks about it, we all are familiar with a number of birthday songs. After all, any song about the Nativity is in a true sense about the birth of Jesus.

Part of the charm of the carol "The Birthday of a King" is its ingenuous yet appropriately descriptive title. Written by William Harold Neidlinger (1863-1924), a Brooklyn-born conductor, composer, organist, and teacher, the song has several traits in common with the ubiquitous "Happy Birthday to You." Neidlinger's song, created about 1890, has an almost identical date and is also especially suitable for children. Most of all, like "Happy Birthday to You," it continues to live on, generation after generation, both because of its popular appeal and because of its serviceability as a special occasion song. It survives partly because at every Christmastide it reminds us that, indeed, Christmas is the birthday of a king!

# A Boy Is Born in Bethlehem

Through most of the Middle Ages, Christmas songs were written only in the languages of the two dominant medieval churches, with Greek carols used by the Eastern church and Latin carols used by the Roman church. Late in the medieval era, around the thirteenth century, carols in the everyday language of common people began to appear. As these popular-language carols became more and more prevalent, new Greek and Latin carols became more and more a rarity. By around the sixteenth century, that is, around the height of the Renaissance, the old-style church-language carols were seldom composed. There were some exceptions to this trend, of which the great eighteenth-century Latin carol "Adeste fideles" ("O Come All Ye Faithful") is the most notable, but as a whole the modern era extinguished the continuance of the old carol genres.

A number of medieval and early modern Latin carols are still actively sung in the twentieth century. One of these is the anonymous fourteenth-century song "Puer natus in Bethlehem," which may have been written in Germany or the adjacent Bohemia region of Czechoslovakia. Although it is not familiar today to most people, and is not even the most frequently sung Latin carol from its era, it is in at least one way the most important carol of its type. Possibly the most culturally influential Christmas song of all time, the lyrics to "Puer natus" have been borrowed for carols in German, Danish, Dutch, and several other languages. Its tune, furthermore, has been widely used, including for other carols and for a well-known harmonization by Johann Sebastian Bach (1685-1750). (Actually, by the sixteenth century the original tune had been supplanted by its descant, or accompanying melody, and that is the form known today.)

Its influential historical role can also be strongly inferred by the abundance of English translations that have been made. All of these English versions are similar–"A Boy Is Born in Bethlehem," "A

Boy Was Born in Bethlehem," "A Child Is Born in Bethlehem," etc. This flock of translations together with its herd of artistic relations suggests that "Puer natus" has been a carol of greatness. Its current slight popularity precludes that status today, but it would certainly be appropriate to describe this old carol as a truly great song of the past.

# Bring a Torch, Jeannette, Isabella

"Who were Jeannette and Isabella?" may not rank high among the literary mysteries of the world, yet the identities of these two famous unknown women do provide an intriguing puzzle for the lighthearted speculator. Were they sisters, daughters, wives, or lovers? Or were they simply names that the poet chose because of sound and/or rhythm?

Although the mystery of these carol characters will never be solved, there is nothing secret about the very high quality of this delightful seventeenth-century folk carol from the Provence region of France. Originally "Un flambeau, Jeannette, Isabelle," it has been honored by a number of English versions, of which "Bring a Torch, Jeannette, Isabella" by Englishman Edward Cuthbert Nunn (1868-1914) is the most popular.

The mysteries associated with the carol do not end with Jeannette and Isabella. There is some cause to believe that the author of the song was Nicholas Saboly (1614-1675), who also may have been the creator of another carol, "Touro-louro-luoro!," which was from the same place and period. In any case, the imaginative lyrics depicting the utilization of torches to light the way to the manger scene and the sprightly and rhythmic melody are a singularly compelling combination. "Bring a Torch" is one of those songs in the category which could be designated as "great lesser-known carols." That is, its esthetics surpass its international appreciation and recognition.

# The Child Jesus

No area on the Earth has a more turbulent combination of history and weather than the Caribbean. Pirates, treasure hunters, dictators, hurricanes, and other disturbing phenomena have been commonplace since Christopher Columbus first discovered the region in the late fifteenth century. Yet all has not been foment and agitation in this tropical environment, for many movements of peaceful creativity have occurred.

One of the islands of the Caribbean which has had its share of artistic activity is the Commonwealth of Puerto Rico. That island has possibly produced more good Christmas songs than any other place in the region. Persons in the United States are familiar with Jose Feliciano's 1970 song "Feliz Navidad" which reportedly is based on a Puerto Rican folk song. Other popular carols are "De tierra lejana venimos" ("Song of the Wise Men"), "Pastores a Belén" ("Shepherds in Bethlehem") and "El Mino Jesus" ("The Child Jesus"). Discounting Feliciano's song as being equally of United States and Puerto Rican origin, "El Mino Jesus" (also called "El Santo Niño" and "El Niño Jesus)" is perhaps the leading carol of its culture.

This folk carol is probably from the late nineteenth or early twentieth century. The lyrics have been attributed to the prominent Spanish poet Antonio Machado (1875-1939), which is a distinct tribute to the quality of the carol, but it is doubtful that Machado was in any way responsible. There is an indirect relationship between "El Mino" and Spain, though. The charming artistic portrayal of the baby Jesus standing at the door is not unique to this carol. Two somewhat similar folk carols, "A esta puerta llama un Niño" and "Madre, en la puerta hay un Niño," which both roughly translate as "There's a Child at the Door," also exist in Spain. Good ideas, it seems, are not confined by national boundaries.

# Coventry Carol

During the Middle Ages, the community of Coventry, England, experienced three very dissimilar events which have not succumbed to the obscuring onslaught of the centuries. The most famous, or rather the most notorious, of these occurred in the eleventh century. Lady Godiva, who was the wife of Leofric, Earl of Mercia, became legendary when she reportedly rode naked on a white horse through the city in exchange for her husband's promise to ease the tax burden of the people. The second event, also with positive and negative features, is the construction of the Cathedral of St. Michael in the fourteenth century. Unfortunately, part of the cathedral's fame has come from its destruction, along with the rest of central Coventry, in an extended air raid by the German Luftwaffe in November 1940.

The third event is the creation of the beloved old song, "Coventry Carol," during the fifteenth century. The mournful lyrics, "Lully, lulla, you little tiny child" (which have several variations), were written for the Pageant of the Shearmen and Tailors in Coventry. (The pageant was a medieval-style mystery play based on biblical stories. At least in the beginning, the pageant was connected with the two guilds.) The lilting melody, probably also composed for the same production, appears to be from the same period. No person has been associated with the authorship of the lyrics except that the oldest known text was written down by Robert Croo in 1534. Likewise, there has been no personal attribution of the compelling melody, whose oldest known printing dates from 1591.

There is, of course, a positive and negative dichotomy with this Coventry event, too. The positive is the lovely and sensitive carol that has come down to us. The negative is the depressing theme of the song, the slaughter of the innocents by Herod. It is highly fortunate that few carols have dealt with this topic, which is the only really unpleasant element of the Christmas story.

# From Heaven Above to Earth I Come

Five landmark events or historical forces occurred around the year 1500. The capture of Constantinople by the Ottoman Turks in 1453 symbolically marked the end of the Middle Ages. The discovery of America in 1492 by Christopher Columbus was the highlight of the geographical revolution of the fifteenth century. The invention of printing with movable type by Johann Gutenberg around 1440-1450 initiated the communications revolution. In 1500 the intellectual revolution, the Renaissance, was in mid-stride, and in 1517 Martin Luther's posting of the 95 theses initiated the Protestant Reformation, or the religious revolution.

Luther (1483-1546) was one of the most prominent persons of the sixteenth century. The Reformation which he led and its multifarious side effects dominated the history of Europe for about 130 years. Yet in spite of enough activities to saturate several lifetimes, Luther found enough time to write some hymns of note. His most important hymn was "Ein feste Burg ist unser Gott" ("A Mighty Fortress Is Our God"), which was written in 1527 or 1528. "Ein feste Burg," still one of the very favorite hymns in Protestant churches, has been called "the battle hymn of the Reformation" and "The Marseillaise . . . of the Reformation."

Luther also composed one original Christmas carol, "Vom Himmel hoch, da komm ich her." Most of his association with carols is peripheral, for example, his translating some carols from the Latin and adding some verses to the fourteenth-century German folk carol "Gelobet seist du, Jesu Christ." (The attribution of "Away in a Manger" to Luther is, incidentally, entirely spurious.) The lyrics for "Vom Himmel hoch" reportedly were written for a Christmas Eve ceremony for Luther's son Hans, in which seven verses were sung by a man dressed as an angel, and the remainder of the 15 verses were sung in response by Luther's children. The year of this incident was most likely 1534. The verses were published in 1535 accompanied by an old German folk melody. Four years later, in 1539, Luther published the carol with a different tune. The new tune, which was probably composed by Luther, was the beautiful melody that has made this carol one of the very favorite Christmas songs in Germany and also one of the better-known carols throughout the world. Of carols created entirely in Germany, it is perhaps rivaled in international recognition only by "O Tannenbaum" ("O Christmas Tree").

Indicative of the tune's wide public acceptance is its utilization for various other purposes. Luther himself wrote a shorter substitute for "Vom Himmel hoch" to be used with his tune. In 1543 he devised the song "Vom Himmel kam der Engel Schar" ("From Heaven Came the Angel Host"), a sort of mini-variant of the 1534 carol which never really caught the attention of audiences. The tune also has been connected with at least four other hymns, plus the English carol, "The Holy Son of God" by Henry More (1614-1687). The ultimate compliment perhaps is its use by the great Johann Sebastian Bach (1685-1750), in three different harmonizations, in his 1734 Christmas Oratorio.

The text of the carol has not had the same happy fate as the melody. Although very skillful in the German original, the words have not really received an outstanding English translation. Of the 15 or 20 translation efforts, the best-known one is probably "From Heaven Above to Earth I Come" by Catherine Winkworth (1827-1878), which was published in 1855. The difficulties with the translation no doubt have limited the carol's popularity in English-speaking countries where it is not one of the highest-ranking or universally familiar songs of the holiday season. Also, the tune, although a very fine one, is not as accessible or catchy as some of the other leading carols.

Two anecdotes help illustrate the historical significance of "From Heaven Above." Reportedly, the carol was sung by a German soldier in response to a French soldier's rendition of the French carol "Cantique de Noël" ("O Holy Night") during a holiday interlude in the Franco-Prussian War of 1870-1871. Of greater cultural implication is a 1931 event in which "Vom Himmel hoch" was sung by 5,000 French Roman Catholics in the Basilica of the

Sacred Heart in Paris. Imagine! French Catholics in great numbers singing a carol by the German leader of the Protestant Reformation.

In the same symbolic spirit that designated Luther's "Ein fest Burg" as "the battle hymn of the Reformation," his only Christmas song should receive a similar epithet. It does not seem at all inappropriate to describe "From Heaven Above" as nothing less than "the carol of the Reformation."

# He Is Born, the Holy Child

Two of the better-known French-language carols are "The March of the Kings" ("La marche des rois) and "He Is Born, the Holy Child" ("Il est né, le divin Enfant"). Both of these songs deal with religious topics of Christmas, both are folk creations from France, both have a positive outlook, and both are famous. Yet it would be difficult to find many other songs with so much in common that have such drastically contrasting natures. "March" is so vital, lively, and full-bodied. "He Is Born" is so timid, reserved, and delicate.

And if one had to make a judgment based entirely on the characteristics of the music to determine which song was the older, it is quite possible that "He Is Born" would be selected. That choice, however, would be a mistake! "March" may sound to some ears as the newer piece, but it was actually created five centuries earlier than "He Is Born." A comparison of the linguistic elements of both carols reveals the relative youth of "He Is Born." When the antiquated lyrics of "March" are placed side by side with those of "He Is Born," the probable eighteenth-century origins of "He Is Born," in contrast to the thirteenth-century origins of "March," become evident.

Overall, though, the reaction to "He Is Born" might be that it seems a bit out of place in the eighteenth century, especially when it is placed side by side with some other French songs of the same period. "Les anges dans nos campagnes" ("Angels We Have Heard on High"), "Patapan," and even the earlier carol "Un flambeau, Jeannette, Isabelle" ("Bring a Torch, Jeannette, Isabella"), all give the impression of being later. But then, a touch of incongruity should not be surprising from a carol whose tune is called "La tête bizarre" (apparent translation, The Bizarre Head).

# He Smiles Within His Cradle

The sight of a smiling baby is one of the more pleasant experiences of human existence. The carol title "He Smiles Within His Cradle" is one of the more delightful formulations of words by any Christmas lyricist. Crafted by the renowned English poet, novelist, and critic Robert Graves (1895-1985 ), who is possibly best known for his novel, *I, Claudius,* "He Smiles Within His Cradle" (or simply "The Cradle") is a fine translation of the sixteenth-century Austrian folk carol "Ein Kindlein in der Wiegen."

Matching Graves's exceptional translation, and other good translations such as "A Babe Lies in the Cradle" and "A Baby in the Cradle," is an equally exceptional tune that has not received as much attention as it merits. It has gained sufficient recognition, though, to have been utilized as a melody for the moderately well-known carol "The World's Desire," whose lyricist was the prestigious English writer G. K. Chesterton (1874-1936).

A third name connected with "He Smiles" is David Gregorius Corner (1585-1648). Because he printed the song in a 1649 Viennese collection, he has been commonly attributed as its author. Unfortunately for Corner, his flirtation with fame has fallen short, for the song was published in 1590 when Corner was a mere "Kind" of five. Yet Corner did make a major contribution to the propagation of this song, which may be the best Austrian carol prior to the composition of the immensely popular "Silent Night" in 1818.

# In the Bleak Mid-Winter

Christina Rossetti (1830-1894) is distinctive because she may be the most accomplished female poet ever to have manipulated the English language in the long literary history of Great Britain. She is additionally distinctive because she is one of the few persons to have produced the lyrics for more than one famous Christmas song in the centuries-old tradition of carol creation. Her two contributions to the genre are "Love Came Down at Christmas" (1885) and "In the Bleak Mid-Winter" (1872).

"Mid-Winter" is quite interesting as a literary piece, with such chilling imagery as "Frosty wind made moan," "Earth stood hard as iron," and "Snow on snow," making it one of the more unusual sets of carol verses. Coupled with Rossetti's verbal descriptions is a very popular melody by the English classical composer Gustav Holst (1874-1934), who is most noted for his orchestral masterpiece "The Planets" (1914-1916), and who also wrote a 1919 tune for the fifteenth-century English folk carol "Lullay My Liking." Holst's tune for "Mid-Winter," published in 1906, is a substantial and original piece of music but also is a bit of a dilemma. If there were a contest for the dreariest melody in a well-liked carol, there would be no doubt as to the winner. Yet to some persons at least, this very mournfulness appears to be part of the carol's appeal. And it does go with the forlorn mood of the first verse. The later verses, however, seem less compatible with the tune, particularly the excellent final stanza which begins with "What can I give him, Poor as I am?"

Almost a century after Rossetti's inspiration, a definite compliment was indirectly given to her work, and possibly to the carol as a whole. In 1963, American Paul Francis Webster (1909-1984), who wrote several popular Christmas songs, published a carol beginning "What can I give him, Poor as I am?"

# Jesus Holy, Born So Lowly

In 1795, as a result of three partitions of its territory, Poland ceased to exist as a political jurisdiction. Because of the powerless status in the late eighteenth century and Poland's relative weakness since that time, it would be completely understandable if there were a widely held opinion that it never was a powerful nation. However, historians know that as few as two centuries before the limbo of 1795, Poland was in fact one of the most powerful and influential countries in Europe. From about the fourteenth through the sixteenth century, in close alliance with Lithuania, Poland held sway over an empire that reached from the Baltic Sea to the Black Sea.

This era, particularly the sixteenth century, was the golden age of Poland. One of the minicultural events that contributed to this golden age was the creation of a significant group of good Christmas carols. The earliest Polish carol of note, "W zlobie lezy," dates from the thirteenth or fourteenth century. This very fine manger song, variously translated as "Jesus Holy, Born So Lowly," "Baby Jesus, in a Manger," "Infant Holy, Infant Lowly," "He Is Sleeping in a Manger," and others, is perhaps the best-known Polish carol. (A somewhat later song, "Lulajze Jezuniu" ["Polish Lullaby"], also strongly vies for this honor.) Another distinction for "Jesus Holy" is its frequent inclusion in hymnals, an event relatively uncommon for carols of simple folk parentage.

# O Bethlehem!

Most persons probably have never heard a Basque carol or have not realized they have done so. Many persons probably are not even aware that Basque carols even exist. Yet an appreciable literature of Christmas music has been created in the Basque regions of northern Spain and southern France. It is not at all surprising that Basque carols are generally obscure, for the Basques, with a very distinct and very old culture and a unique language, are possibly the least understood important ethnic group in Europe. Despite their relative isolation from their neighbors and their relatively small population, these independent and fervently Roman Catholic people have contributed significantly to the histories of Spain and France and have produced prominent personages such as St. Ignatius of Loyola and St. Francis Xavier.

"O Bethlehem!" (in Basque "Oi! Betleem!" or "Oi Betlehem"), a good nativity carol with English versions by several translators, is perhaps the best-known carol by the Basques. Other Basque carols of note are "Companions, All Sing Loudly" or "We Sing of David's Daughter" ("Khanta zagun guziek"), "Lovely Baby Mary Bore Him," ("Aur txiki"), "Who Were the Shepherds, Mary?" ("Etzen bada Maria?"), and "In Middle Winter They Set Out" ("Belen'en sortu zaigu"). The quality of melodies in Basque carols is not only evident in these songs, but in the several non-Basque carols which have utilized Basque tunes. This latter category includes the moderately well-known carols, "Gabriel's Message" and "The Infant King" (words for both by Englishman Sabine Baring-Gould [1834-1924]) plus "Lullay My Liking" (a fifteenth-century English folk carol). So the next time you think of Christmas music, devote at least a modicum of your reflection to the obscure but not unproductive Basque people.

# O Come, Little Children

A variety of well-known carols have been specifically written for children, including some like "O Little Town of Bethlehem" and "Jingle Bells," which are enjoyed by people in every age group. Very few Christmas songs, however, have been specifically written about children, exempting, of course, the fact that the full purpose of Christmas is the observance of the birth of the child Jesus. The best example of a carol with children as a primary topic could well be the nineteenth-century German song, "Ihr Kindelein, kommet" ("O Come, Little Children"). Not only is it almost surely the most famous carol about children, but the background of its poet is in large part compatible with the nature of its theme.

Christoph von Schmid (1768-1854) was a German Roman Catholic priest and schoolmaster who devoted much of his effort to children, including the production of an extensive amount of literature for younger readers that spanned a couple of generations. In the earlier part of his life (1801) he published *Biblische Geschichte fur die Kinder (Bible Stories for Children)* and near the end of his many years he authored "Ihr Kindelein, kommet" (around 1850 or somewhat before). Schmid's verses were set to a melody by Johann Abraham Peter Schulz (1747-1800). A German by birth, Schulz was a well-traveled conductor, composer, and organist who probably wrote the tune during his tenure at the court of the King of Denmark during the period from 1787 to 1795.

Schulz worked for a king, a princess, and a prince during his career as a musician. Schmid received his preposition of nobility (the "von") in 1837. Yet their carol has none of the trappings and pretentiousness of royalty or nobility. It is quiet, unassuming, and totally lacking in pomposity. In other words, it is an ideal vehicle for its purpose.

# O Little Town of Bethlehem

The land of Palestine, which is the Holy Land for Judaism, Islam, and Christianity, has been visited by countless pilgrims and other travelers. One of these visitors, and one who was deeply affected by the religious meaning of this Middle Eastern crossroads, was the young Episcopal clergyman Phillips Brooks (1835-1893). During December 1865 and January 1866, Brooks spent several weeks in Palestine during his year-long voyage abroad on leave from his church in Philadelphia.

Apparently the sights and events of his sojourn in the Holy Land, especially his attendance at the Christmas service of the Church of the Nativity in Bethlehem, impressed him strongly and indelibly. About three years later the memories of the trip were recalled and inspired him to mold a sensitive and insightful poem, the immortal carol "O Little Town of Bethlehem." This was not the first successful carol by Boston-born Brooks, who in addition to being a carol writer was Episcopal bishop of Massachusetts, an extraordinary orator, the author of many books and articles, and overall one of the most respected and accomplished ministers of the nineteenth-century United States. Between 1862 and 1868, he also wrote the lyrics for the moderately well-known carol "Everywhere, Everywhere, Christmas Tonight."

His 1868 children's carol, though, was to be the centerpiece of his distinguished career. Reportedly, shortly before Christmas in that year Brooks penned some verses to be sung by the Sunday school children at the annual Christmas program of his church, Holy Trinity. Then he asked his friend Lewis H. Redner (1831-1908), a real estate broker who served as Holy Trinity's Sunday school superintendent and organist, to supply a simple setting for the poem. Previously, Redner had collaborated with Brooks on "Everywhere, Everywhere." On this occasion, however, the artistic collaboration almost did not take place. By the time he went to bed the night before the Christmas program, Redner had not produced a satisfactory tune. During the night, the story continues, he woke up with "an angel strain" sounding in his ears. He immediately jotted down the melody, which he called "a gift from heaven," and the following morning added the harmony. Later that day, on December 27, 1868, the children inaugurated the modest yet soon to be great classic of the Christmas season.

This carol-creating episode matches the romanticism of the famous events leading to the composition of "Silent Night." The popularity of "O Little Town," furthermore, approaches that of its most illustrious Austrian counterpart. It is the best-known American religious carol, challenged slightly by "It Came upon the Midnight Clear." In the late twentieth-century United States the secular carols "White Christmas" and "Jingle Bells" are surely more popular, but on an international basis perhaps no American carol exceeds "O Little Town" in acceptance.

Yet in spite of the song's high degree of fame, which is due to exceptional lyrics that mesh so effectively with refined, tasteful, graceful, and well-structured music, the carol is often printed in other than its original form. For some uncertain reason, Redner's outstanding tune has more than occasionally been replaced by lesser melodies, particularly in Great Britain. The principal alternate is "The Ploughboy's Dream" (also called "Forest Green"), an English folk song which was substituted by the eminent English composer Ralph Vaughan Williams (1872-1958) in the 1906 collection, *The English Hymnal.* Since the carol with Redner's tune had been published as early as 1874, and also had been included in the American Episcopal church's 1892 collection, *The Church Hymnal,* it is doubtful that the music editor of an Anglican hymnal would be unfamiliar with the original melody. More likely, Vaughan Williams simply decided to promote one of the folk tunes of which he was a strong proponent. Other tunes, including one by Henry Walford Davies (1869-1941), which was written expressly for "O Little Town," and one by Joseph Barnby (1838-1896), have been attached to the lyrics; only Redner's tune and Vaughan Williams' "Forest Green" are used to much extent.

As so often happens, it was only by two quirks of fate that the carol was brought to life. One of these was the legendary visit of the angels to Lewis Redner. The other was an 1864 event in which Redner would have left his position as organist because of an excessive work load except for the persuasion of his colleague Brooks. If either of these incidents had taken a negative turn, Redner's place in cultural history would have been minuscule, and one of the most celebrated and most performed carols of all time would never have been conceived. All this favorable treatment by fate plus the carol's superior artistry makes one almost believe Redner's claim of angelic intervention.

# Once in Royal David's City

Virtually all of the favorite songs of the holiday season have something particularly unusual in their nature, history, or relationships. There is one carol, on the other hand, which could best be characterized by the strange-sounding epithet "exceptional only by being unexceptional." The recipient of this dubious distinction is "Once in Royal David's City," which is about as bland and unexciting as any famous carol could be.

The creator of the lyrics, Englishwoman Cecil Frances Alexander (1823-1895), led a pretty placid life. Besides being the author of the 1848 carol and several other respected hymns, and being the wife of the primate of Ireland, there was nothing especially dramatic, extraordinary, or attention-getting in her 72 years on Earth. Perhaps her finest achievement was the lyrics for the outstanding 1848 hymn "All Things Bright and Beautiful," which were the inspiration for James Herriot's novel *All Creatures Great and Small* and subsequent works about the life of a country veterinarian in Yorkshire.

The lyrics for Alexander's carol, in contrast, are not at the top of the Christmas music genre, though good. In part this is because the words were simple and not complex, being written for children.

Similarly, the music, though pleasant and competent, is neither especially popular nor esthetic. The 1849 tune by Englishman Henry John Gauntlett (1805-1876) does not rank among the best of carol melodies. His life, furthermore, is not any more interesting than Mrs. Alexander's. He was an organist and organ builder besides being the composer of about 10,000 hymn tunes, of which this carol is by far the most familiar. Overall, the only really intriguing elements about this song are the names of its creators. "Cecil," which is almost exclusively a male name, belonged in this instance to a female, and "Gauntlett" is the type of surname upon which puns could very easily be inflicted.

# Polish Lullaby

Frédéric Chopin (1810-1849) is the most talented and accomplished composer of Polish birth. "Lulajze Jezuniu," a folk carol which most likely dates from the late medieval or early modern period (fifteenth-seventeenth century), is one of the finest Christmas songs from Poland. Another shared experience between Chopin and the carol, besides geography, fame, and quality, is Chopin's insertion of the song's melody in his Scherzo in B Minor (1831 or 1832).

Chopin's motivation for inclusion of the tune in his piano work was partly patriotic, for he frequently employed themes from his homeland. One can speculate, however, that much of the reason for his choosing that particular melody was its exceptional artistic merit. For "Lulajze Jezuniu" (in English "Polish Lullaby," "Sleep, Little Jesus," "Rockabye Jesus," and others) may very well be the most famous Polish carol. One other carol, "W zlobie lezy" ("Jesus Holy, Born So Lowly) possibly competes for this honor. But "Polish Lullaby"'s absorption by the genius of Chopin gives it an extra psychological advantage over all contenders.

# Rocking

Carols in the gentle form of lullabies have been used in a wide variety of cultures. "Away in a Manger" from the United States, "El Rorro" ("The Babe") from Mexico, "Lulajze Jezuniu" ("Polish Lullaby") from Poland, "Stille Nacht, heilige Nacht" ("Silent Night") from Austria, and "Hajej, nynjej" ("Rocking") from Czechoslovakia are all examples of notable Christmas songs written in lullaby style. "Rocking" may be the oldest of these carols. Because of this, it may also be regarded as a prototype of its genre.

From folk sources of the late Middle Ages or early modern period (around the fourteenth to the sixteenth century), "Rocking" (also translated as "Rocking Song," "Lullaby," "Little Jesus, Sweetly Sleep," "Rocking Carol," and "Shepherd's Rocking Carol") is perhaps the quintessential lullaby. The terminology of the English translations are all strongly suggestive of this, as is the impression of rocking the cradle which the melody clearly emits. Altogether, it is a modest yet highly successful song, and among Czech carols could only be eclipsed in international acceptance by "Nesem vám noviny" ("Angels and Shepherds").

# The Simple Birth

Agatha Christie's famed fictional detective Hercule Poirot was almost invariably upset when he was called "French." The reaction of the brilliant but egotistical sleuth is completely understandable because indeed he was not French, but Belgian. And quite possibly the root cause for his response to misidentification is the propensity for the culture of his native country to be linked with those of its neighbors, France and the Netherlands. The salient example of this cultural confusion may be the language situation in Belgium. One of the two major languages is French and the other is Flemish which is considered to be either a Dutch dialect or a very close relative of Dutch.

Even the carols of Belgium are often hard to differentiate from those of France and the Netherlands. But there are some internationally known carols that clearly originated in the land of Hercule Poirot. The two most popular ones seem to be "De drie koningen" ("The Three Kings"), a folk song possibly from the fifteenth or sixteenth century, and "De nederige geboorte" ("The Simple Birth"), another folk song from perhaps the same period. If either of these is dominant, it would be "The Simple Birth," a superior early nativity song. It has received at least five English translations, including versions entitled "A Little Child on the Earth Has Been Born" (derived from the first line), and "Flemish Carol." The latter title possibly exemplifies the cultural identity syndrome of the Belgians, for it could be interpreted as suggesting that the song is the one and only Flemish carol of significance.

# Sleep, My Little Jesus

The number two runs throughout the history of the affable lullaby "Sleep, My Little Jesus." Its composer was one of two blind musicians to create a carol of note. The other was Henry Thomas Smart (1813-1879), who a few years after he went blind composed the music for the more renowned "Angels from the Realms of Glory." "Sleep"'s composer was also one of two residents of Philadelphia to create the music for a carol of note. The other was Lewis Henry Redner (1831-1908), who composed the music for the more renowned "O Little Town of Bethlehem." "Sleep"'s lyricist was one of two Unitarian ministers to write the words for a carol of note. The other was Edmund Hamilton Sears (1810-1876), who penned the verses for the more renowned "It Came upon the Midnight Clear." In all these categories, "Sleep, My Little Jesus" was consistently number two.

The musician was Adam Geibel (1855-1933), a blind German-born composer, organist, and publisher who spent most of his life in the Philadelphia area. In addition to "Sleep, My Little Jesus," Geibel is also known for the composition of the hymn "Stand Up, Stand Up for Jesus." The poet was William Channing Gannett (1840-1923), a Boston-born hymnist and hymn compiler. He published the lyrics in 1894 when he was pastor of the Unitarian Church in Rochester, New York. They had been written, however, in 1882, when he was living in the Minneapolis-St. Paul area, the twin cities region. Again, the number two appears.

# The Sleep of the Infant Jesus

One's view of anything is greatly altered by the perspective from which it is observed. This truism applies to carols no less than other elements in our experiences. The best example of the effect of perspective on a Christmas song may well be the pleasant eighteenth-century French folk carol "Le sommeil de l'enfant Jesus," which is possibly from the Anjou region.

The French title and its several English translations, such as "The Sleep of the Infant Jesus," "The Sleep of the Child Jesus," and "Slumber Song of the Infant Jesus," all connote an aura of delicacy and gentility. However, when the focus of attention shifts to the variant French title of the same song, a much different impression is created. The French original of the variant, "Entre le boeuf et l'âne gris," and its several translations such as "Shelter Where Ox and Ass Are One," "'Twixt Gentle Ox and Ass So Gray," and "Here Betwixt Ass and Oxen Mild," present a much more earthy and mundane picture. Whichever of these titles happens to be available to the carol performer or listener could well color the reaction to the song. Yet no matter what the wording of the title may be, the carol itself remains essentially the same. It might be an interesting psychological test, though, to see if the contrasting slants of the title actually elicit contrasting audience responses.

# The Snow Lay on the Ground

Although much of Europe and North America experiences snow during Christmastide, the crystalline precipitation which is so ubiquitous in northern climates during the winter season is almost nonexistent as a theme in traditional Christmas songs. The only well-known folk carols which directly refer to snow are "O Tannenbaum" ("O Christmas Tree"), "Good King Wenceslas," and "The Snow Lay on the Ground."

With snow so prominently displayed in its title, one might believe that the subject of the last-mentioned carol is the wintertime. In a way it is, but the reference to snow is inappropriate since the event related by the song is the birth of Jesus, which most likely occurred in the springtime. Even if the Nativity did take place in late December, the odds of snow being on the ground in Bethlehem are infinitesimal. In spite of the weather anomaly, however, this carol with its nineteenth-century folk lyrics from the West Country of England and its Irish or English folk melody from roughly the same period remains moderately popular today. Similar to a number of other Christmas songs which have some sort of logical, historical, or artistic deficiencies, the shortcomings of this carol are generally ignored by the celebrants of Christmas. Rather than think about such trivialities, the persons experiencing the song are musically involved in the sacred observance of the holiday. As expressed in the carol's variant title, "Venite adoremus" (derived from the beginning words of the refrain), they are coming to worship the new Christ child.

# Song of the Nuns of Chester

Women's religious orders have been a vital sector of the Roman Catholic church for many centuries. But although some famous carols have been created by men closely affiliated with the church (for example, "'Twas in the Moon of Wintertime," "O Come, Little Children," "O Come All Ye Faithful," "Silent Night," and possibly "In Dulci Jubilo"), women of the church have only tangential and passive connections with two carols of note. A tune used for a fifteenth-century processional sung by Franciscan nuns may have been the source for the music for "O Come, O Come Emmanuel." At about the same period, nuns from Chester, England, were linked with another carol.

Created in the fourteenth or early fifteenth century, the anonymous carol was entitled "Qui creavit coelum" ("He by Whom the Heavens Were Made," "Chester Carol," "Carol of the Nuns of Saint Mary's Chester," and "Song of the Nuns of Chester"). This lovely Latin lullaby utilized by the sisters is one of the typical carols of late medieval England. Yet a century or so later the traits which made it typical, that is, Latin language, strong religious content, and connection with the Catholic church, largely disappeared. It is one of the last Latin carols written in England. A distinguished contemporary, "There Is No Rose of Such Virtue," had already abandoned Latin for English. Even in the still-medieval fifteenth century songs such as "The Boar's Head Carol" had mostly nonreligious lyrics, and by the sixteenth-century highly secular carols such as "We Wish You a Merry Christmas" became commonplace throughout the British Isles. In addition, Henry VIII's break with Rome in 1534 greatly diminished the influence of the Catholic Church in England. Thus the "Song of the Nuns of Chester" is in some ways the benchmark of the passing of an era. But lest we mourn too much, the period which succeeded it was the English Renaissance, the greatest cultural epoch in the history of that nation and also the golden age of the English carol.

# What Child Is This?

King Henry VIII of England (1491-1547) is a figure of both great fame and enormous notoriety. He is well known for his major role in the development of early modern England and in the conversion of England to Protestantism. He is equally well known for his egotism, his indulgent lifestyle, and his many wives. Lesser known, though, was his skill in sports and in music. Among his reputed accomplishments in music are the tunes for the obscure sixteenth-century carol "Green Grow'th the Holly" and for one of the world's most famous songs, "Greensleeves." It is quite possible that Henry composed the tune for "Green Grow'th the Holly" and quite doubtful that he was responsible for "Greensleeves." If this immodest man had written "Greensleeves," it seems unlikely that its "anonymous" label would ever have surfaced. The chances are much better for his being erroneously attributed as the author than for his authorship being overlooked or forgotten. Perhaps the presence of "Green" at the beginning of the titles of both songs was a factor in the genesis of this myth.

Although Henry is probably not the author of "Greensleeves," the song is a product of the sixteenth century. One suspects that this folk classic may have been created in the second half of the century (during the reign of Elizabeth I). In any case, it was mentioned in 1580 and by 1600 was so much a part of the contemporary English culture that it was referred to in Act Two, Scene One of Shakespeare's *The Merry Wives of Windsor*. Over the centuries the melody has been widely utilized, including use as a party song by the supporters of Charles I during the English Civil War (1642-1648), as a part of John Gay's *The Beggar's Opera* (1728), as the tune for the seventeenth-century folk carol "The Old Year Now Away Is Fled," and as the tune for the well-known nineteenth-century carol "What Child Is This?"

The lyrics for "What Child Is This?" were written around 1865 by Englishman William Chatterton Dix (1837-1898). By vocation an insurance executive and by avocation a poet, Dix was also the creator of two other carol lyrics of note, "Like Silver Lamps in a Distant Shrine" (1871) and "As with Gladness Men of Old" (1859). It is unknown who brought Dix's lyrics and "Greensleeves" together, but quite possibly it was John Stainer (1840-1901), who made a harmonization. Except perhaps for the original words for "Greensleeves," which begin "Alas my love, ye do me wrong," the very competent verses by Dix are the lyrics most used with the exquisite, sensitive, and haunting sixteenth-century melody. Since Christmas is such an important holiday, with an enormous entourage of music, it is more than a little satisfying to have "Greensleeves," one of the most beloved pieces of music in Western civilization, as a prominent member of the Christmas musical tradition.

# MARY AND JOSEPH

# Ave Maria

The celebrated Viennese composer Franz Schubert (1797-1828) is famous for what he did not finish, that is, his "Unfinished" Symphony No. 8 (1822). He is also famous for what he did finish, including the spiritual and very beautiful song "Ave Maria." Written in April 1825, "Ave Maria" (or "Hail Mary") was substantially inspired by the 1810 poem "The Lady of the Lake." That well-known composition was from the creative mind of Sir Walter Scott (1771-1832), who is best remembered for his historical novels such as *Ivanhoe*.

Two facets of "Ave Maria" are quite conducive to confusion. First, there have been many musical compositions called "Ave Maria," of which the one by Schubert and an 1859 creation by French composer Charles Gounod (1818-1893), adapted from Johann Sebastian Bach, are the most popular. (Gounod is most noted for his 1859 opera, *Faust*, but fans of Alfred Hitchcock's long-running television series are very familiar with another Gounod piece, "Funeral March of a Marionette," [1872], which was Hitchcock's theme song.) Second, "Ave Maria" (either the Schubert or the Gounod) is only by the most liberal interpretation a Christmas song. It is actually a Roman Catholic prayer to the Virgin Mary based partly on a passage from the Gospel of Luke. But the Schubert and Gounod versions are sometimes included in Christmas collections or medleys partly because of their theme about Mary and partly because their devout temperament and exquisite renderings are most compatible with the sacred foundations of Christmas.

# Blessed Be That Maid Marie

Perhaps the most fascinating personal name affiliated with a Christmas song is that of William Ballet. Since little is known about this man except that he flourished in England around 1600, there is some reason to doubt the authenticity of this picturesque nomenclature. "William" or "Will" can be frequently found in the history and legend of medieval and early modern England. There was William the Conqueror, of course, and Will Scarlet, the companion of Robin Hood, and the eternal will-o'-the-wisp. A contemporary namesake of William Ballet indeed, was no less than the very famous yet somewhat unknown William Shakespeare. In the same way that all sorts of romantic connotations can be read into the name of the great bard, e.g., "Shakespear," the actor who played supporting roles, similar impressions can be gained from "Ballet," the musician. Only a few years before 1600, ballet had become a popular topic in European cultural circles. In 1581 a landmark dance work, *Le ballet comique de la Reine*, was produced in France and in 1588 the first treatise on ballet dancing was published. This latter work, incidentally, is also noted for first printing the melody for the carol "Ding Dong! Merrily on High."

Whether or not the name William Ballet was real or pseudonymous, the person known by that name was directly or indirectly responsible for two good and enduring carols about Mary. The first is "Blessed Be That Maid Marie." The carol's lyrics are folk verses probably from the fifteenth or sixteenth century, and its tune is probably sixteenth-century folk. The tune was first printed in Ballet's *Lute Book* (around 1600). Since Ballet is known to be the author of both words and music for another carol, "Sweet Was the Song the Virgin Sang" (also around 1600), there is cause to suspect that he may have also composed the music for "Blessed Be That Maid Marie."

# The Cherry Tree Carol

There is no such song as "The Cherry Tree Carol." References to it help to perpetuate a myth. Unfortunately, though, the myth is so widely sustained that it may never be dispelled. The truth of the matter is that there are a number of "Cherry Tree" carols so that instead of the very misleading singular form a multiple designation such as "The Cherry Tree Carols," or even better, "The Cherry Tree Carol Series" should be substituted.

The original "Cherry Tree Carol" was a trio of English folk songs apparently from the fifteenth or sixteenth century. The first part of the collective entity was "Joseph Was an Old Man," the second part was "As Joseph Was A-Walking," and the third part was "Mary's Question," an Easter song. Related to their English cousins are at least five distinct American songs with the cherry tree motif. From Kentucky or the Appalachian region are two carols entitled "Joseph and Mary" (an English song of the same title is unrelated) and single carols entitled "The Cherry Tree," "When Joseph Was an Old Man," and "Oh, Joseph Took Mary Up on His Right Knee." These five are probably from the eighteenth or nineteenth century. All of the seven Christmas songs have different tunes, but some have multiple tunes and/or tunes used for other cherry tree carols.

"The Cherry Tree Carol" is the most hilarious phenomenon in the Christmas repertory, although its creators were almost certainly quite serious. Its story tells of Joseph and Mary walking through a cherry orchard which has "cherries and berries so red as any blood" and how the cherry trees bowed down to Mary so that she could eat them. Eventually, by the second part, Christmas becomes a direct subject of the song when Joseph goes walking and encounters an angel who sings about the upcoming birth of Jesus. All of the cherry tree carols touch upon these literary fantasies. But there is such a variety of lyrics and so many musical variants that carol audiences are frequently confused about this batch of similarly named songs which may seem to be as numerous as the fruit on the allegorical tree. It would be difficult to educate holiday celebrants about all the possible variations they might face, but with the knowledge that multiple songs exist they might be much less surprised when they encounter a stranger with a friend's name. Armed with such a piece of information, they might be able to dispel this musical myth just as the cherry tree-chopping myth associated with George Washington has more or less been cut down to size.

# I Sing of a Maiden

Five centuries separate the words and usual music of this delicate old carol. In fifteenth-century England, still in the medieval period, some talented folk poet penned the verses for "I Sing of a Mayden That Is Makeles" or "As Dew in Aprille." In the twentieth century, at least six composers have created musical settings for the early poem, and one or another of these melodies is typically the music utilized for the carol today.

The list of composers that have considered the verses as being worthwhile of their musical efforts is indeed impressive. The names include the great English musicians Martin Shaw (1875-1958) and Benjamin Britten (1913-1976), the prominent English carol historian, compiler, and composer Sir Richard Runciman Terry (1865-1938), and three lesser-known persons, David Farquhar (1928- ), Patrick Hadley (1899- ), and Lennox Berkely (1903- ). (Shaw's version may be the best.) This array of musicians associated with "I Sing of a Maiden" strongly suggests their appreciation of the sensitivity and the quality of the late-medieval lyrics. Like the variant title, the carol is as soft and fragile as dew in April. Like the main title, the carol is one of the more makeles (matchless) songs of its era.

# Joseph, Dearest Joseph Mine

Many carols mention or imply Mary in their titles. Few mention Joseph. The several compositions in the collective entity called "The Cherry Tree Carol" and the late medieval German carol, "Joseph, Dearest Joseph Mine" ("Joseph, lieber Joseph mein"), are the only widely known Christmas songs which devote much attention to Mary's husband.

The lyrics for "Joseph, Dearest" were created anonymously in the fourteenth or fifteenth century. By the late fifteenth century, they were linked with a very lovely anonymous tune which probably was composed in fourteenth-century Germany. One of the carol's earliest appearances was in a mystery play, that most fascinating medieval theatrical institution. Before it was affiliated with "Joseph, Dearest," the exceptional tune was also attached to the well-known Latin carol from thirteenth- or fourteenth-century Germany, "Resonet in laudibus."

With the combination of clever lyrics, which relate a conversation between Mary and Joseph concerning rocking the baby Jesus and singing to him, and one of the very best melodies from the Middle Ages, "Joseph, Dearest" is among the finest carol products of the premodern era. Even if the song should unfortunately leave our modern carol repertory, its music may well survive in one of the other roles to which it has been adapted. The German composer Peter Cornelius (1824-1874) integrated the melody into his Christmas song cycle "Christkind." And the German master Johannes Brahms (1833-1897) blended the melody into his song "Geistliches Wiegenlied" ("Spiritual Cradle Song").

# Lo, How a Rose E'er Blooming

The golden age of the Christmas carol was the sixteenth century, and to a lesser extent the fifteenth century. The nineteenth century could, in another way, stake claim to this honor because of the abundance of carol collecting, translating, arranging, publishing, and related activities accomplished during that epoch on top of the composition of some well-known carols. In creative spirit, however, no period can match the late Middle Ages and Renaissance.

The fifteenth century is definitely less than the great sixteenth century in its carol products, but the earlier era also has contributed strongly to the history of the genre. Among the notable carols composed in or around the fifteenth century are the English carols "I Saw Three Ships," "Coventry Carol," "The Boar's Head Carol," "The Cherry Tree Carol," "I Sing of a Maiden," and "There Is No Rose of Such Virtue," and "Listen Lordlings, Unto Me" (a folk piece most commonly attached to a sixteenth-century folk tune from Gascony, France), the Dutch carol "Jesus' Bloemhof" ("The Garden of Jesus"), the French song "Celebrons la naissance" ("We Sing in Celebration"), and the German carols "Joseph, lieber Joseph mein" ("Joseph, Dearest Joseph Mine"), and "Es ist ein Ros' entsprungen" ("Lo, How a Rose E'er Blooming").

The last-mentioned folk song is among the very best of its era, and in fact is one of the better carols of all time. This high rating could be inferred from its continued use in modern hymnals (a role infrequently accorded to folk songs) and by the at least 12 English translations that have been devised. By far the most familiar translation is "Lo, How a Rose E'er Blooming" which was authored by American Theodore Baker (1851-1934) of *Baker's Biographical Dictionary of Musicians* fame. Some other translations are "There Is a Flower," "I Know a Flower," "Behold, a Lovely Flower," "A Noble Flower of Juda," "The Noble Stem of Jesse," "I Know a Rose Tree Springing," "Behold a Branch Is Growing," and the quaint title, "The World's Fair Rose."

The rose imagery of this carol, which is by no means unusual in its era, is an allusion to Mary as a blooming plant. Ironically, this excellent allegorical device may have delayed the publication of the carol. After the beginning of the Reformation in the sixteenth century, songs dealing with Mary were either ignored or altered by the Lutherans. In this instance the former option was apparently exercised. Despite the adversities posed by the Reformation and by a delay in publication of as much as two centuries, "Lo, How a Rose" survived because of its well-crafted lyrics and, most of all, because of its limited-range yet passionate and exquisite melody. It was not printed until around 1600, though by 1609 it received a tremendous boost when it was harmonized by the famous German composer Michael Praetorius (1571-1621). That arrangement, which is the one most commonly used today, helped considerably in the publicizing of the carol and also led some persons to erroneously attribute the carol to Praetorius.

Of all that could be said or done, perhaps the highest tribute to "Lo, How a Rose" was the adoption of the melody by the great German composer Johannes Brahms (1833-1897) as the basis for an 1896 chorale prelude. To be associated with a master after a four-century interlude is certainly one sign of excellence. To be well-liked and frequently used after five centuries of considerable cultural change is an even clearer indicator.

# The Seven Joys of Mary

The number seven is often regarded as a symbol of good luck. "Seven come eleven" is the hopeful cry of those gambling with dice. Seven is also frequently encountered as a positive element throughout the long history of man and his imagination. Some notable examples are seven days in a week, seven seas, seven hills of Rome, seven-league boots, Seven Wise Men of Greece, Seven Wonders of the World, Seven against Thebes, the Magnificent Seven, Secret Agent 007, seventh sons, and seventh heaven. The joys of the Virgin Mary were also apparently seven in quantity. For that is what the English folk carol "The Seven Joys of Mary" (also known as "The Seven Good Joys," "The Seven Rejoices of Mary," and "Joys Seven") clearly connotes. Its fifteenth-century poem, telling of "The first good joy that Mary had" and so on until seven, is one of the more interesting lyrics of the premodern epoch. Coupled with at least two English folk tunes, one eighteenth century and one probably earlier, it is an effective and enduring late medieval piece. Its historical popularity can be inferred by its use in fifteenth-century English mystery plays and by the mimicking of its concepts by an eighteenth- or nineteenth-century Appalachian folk carol "The Seven Blessings of Mary."

# There Is No Rose of Such Virtue

One thing this anonymous English carol is not exceptional for is its rose theme. From the fourteenth or early fifteenth century, first appearing in a text around 1420, it is in subject matter a typical song of its time. Other contemporary carols also deal with botanical symbolism, including the fifteenth-century German folk classic "Es ist ein Ros' entsprungen" ("Lo, How a Rose E'er Blooming") which similarly features the allegory of Mary as a flower.

Two things for which "There Is No Rose" is exceptional are its staying power and its pioneering qualities. It still receives a degree of attention in the twentieth century including an alternative musical setting by the renowned English composer Benjamin Britten (1913-1976). On the other end of the five- or six-century time spectrum, "There Is No Rose of Such Vertu" (its earliest form) was one of the very first carols to use English as its language instead of Latin. Even though its style and theme are definitely medieval, its preference for the vernacular of the common people makes it to some extent a precursor of the English Renaissance.

# A Virgin Most Pure

With terminology such as "A Virgin Unspotted," "A Virgin Most Blessed," and "A Virgin Most Pure," one could easily believe that this cheerful English folk song is a product of the Middle Ages. Yet in spite of such old-sounding titles, it is at least a century removed from the medieval scene. The words, which were published in 1734, were most likely created in the seventeenth century, possibly in the Gloucestershire region. A number of tunes have been attached to the text, of which perhaps the most popular is a folk melody created about a century later, again possibly in Gloucestershire. A derivative carol also evolved in the Appalachian region, which has been fertile territory for the absorption and modification of English folk carols.

This is not the only modern carol that contains such anachronistic terminology. Two nineteenth-century lyrics, "A Cradle Song of the Blessed Virgin" or "The Virgin Stills the Crying," an 1871 poem by Henry Ramsden Bramley (1833-1917), and "The Virgin's Cradle Hymn," an 1801 poem by Samuel Taylor Coleridge (1772-1837), both have similarly antiquated wording. But both of these were derivatives of probably medieval Latin lyrics and so the impression of early times is understandable. Some black spirituals such as "Virgin Mary Had One Son" also contain similar terminology, but their unsophisticated and spontaneous natures do not make these words seem out of place. "A Virgin Most Pure," in contrast, does appear somewhat ill-at-ease in its chronological context. The degree of inappropriateness becomes more apparent when other well-known English folk carols of roughly the same period are brought to mind. "Wassail Song," "The Holly and the Ivy," and "The Twelve Days of Christmas," which date from the seventeenth and early eighteenth centuries, are in language and mood drastically different from "A Virgin Most Pure." But they are not, we should note, miles apart in artistry.

# ANGELS

## Angels from the Realms of Glory

Any carol which has a great melody is indeed fortunate. A carol with two great melodies, it should then follow, should be doubly blessed. Such is not true for the distinguished carol "Angels from the Realms of Glory." The existence of two excellent musical settings has not enhanced the public acceptance of the carol and to the contrary may have negatively affected its popularity. The reason for this possible problem is that multiple tunes for one set of lyrics have a tendency to decrease recognition potential. This multiple-tune syndrome can also be diagnosed in two other top carols, "Away in a Manger" and "While Shepherds Watched Their Flocks."

The first tune used for "Angels" is the superlative one connected with the eighteenth century French carol, "Les anges dans nos campagnes" ("Angels We Have Heard On High"). That tune apparently was the only music commonly associated with "Angels from the Realms of Glory" for at least 50 years after the lyrics by James Montgomery (1771-1854) were published on December 24, 1816. The five-stanza hymn was first printed in the Sheffield *Iris*, an English newspaper edited by Montgomery. In addition to being a hymn writer and journalist, Montgomery was also a social activist. He was jailed more than once for supporting causes which did not find favor with the government.

In contrast, his exceptional 1816 hymn has been well received by Christmas celebrants throughout the world. The lyrics, the cream of Montgomery's approximately 400 hymns (which include the moderately well-known 1821 carol "Hail to the Lord's Anointed"), are among the very best in the literature of carols. They have even been rated, with some justification, as comparing favorably with any hymn ever written. Yet the carol was not a totally original creation. Montgomery based his stirring poetry on "Les anges dans nos campagnes," or, in other words, he produced a semi-translation or paraphrase of the French carol. In spite of this dependency on "Les anges" and the close linkage with that carol's tune for over half a century, Montgomery's poetry and the French melody do not fit together especially well. The melody for "Les anges" is subtle and delicate, while the lyrics for "Angels from the Realms of Glory" definitely suggest the need for a sweeping and powerful companion. Add to this mismating the blatant incompatibility of the musical rhythm of "Les Anges"'s refrain with the poetic meter of "Angel"'s refrain, and the eventual replacement by a more suitable tune was perhaps inevitable.

In 1867 a melody which possessed all of the necessary characteristics was published in London. Its composer was the accomplished English church musician Henry Thomas Smart (1813-1879), who had gone blind a few years before. At first the tune was attached to another hymn, Horatio Bonar's "Glory Be to God the Father," but after a while it was joined by some unknown person to Montgomery's carol. As time passed, Smart's tune, which ranks in the highest echelon of sacred music, displaced in large part the French tune, although the earlier melody is still widely used in Great Britain. With the newer, more symbiotic combination, the song has become one of the finest pieces of the Christmas season. But despite the superior lyrics blending so well with the highly positive, forceful, and spiritual melody, the carol is not quite as popular as its artistry might suggest. The multiple-tune syndrome possibly could be partially responsible for this. The root cause, though, may be that the song is a little too ecclesiastical, too overwhelming, and/or too involving to fully satisfy the tastes of a mass audience.

# Angels We Have Heard on High

Of the several widespread myths about Christmas carols, the most intriguing is almost surely the amazing Telesphorus tale. The story line of this incredible bit of misinformation relates the singing of a nativity hymn in the year A.D. 129 via the orders of Bishop Telesphorus of Rome. This ancient Latin hymn, the anecdote continues, ultimately evolved into the refrain of the famous French carol "Les anges dans nos campagnes." There are three enormous difficulties with the Telesphorus incident. One is the infinitesimally tiny odds that any piece of music could survive for nearly two millenniums. Another is the total lack of any historical documentation for the incident. And the other is the style of the music in question, which clearly indicates composition in the modern era.

After the myth of Telesphorus and other erroneous data about the carol are cast into the trash can of history, the fragments that remain provide a reasonably certain chronology. The carol is probably a product of eighteenth-century France and is totally anonymous. By 1816 the carol was known in England, for on that date James Montgomery (1771-1854) derived his renowned carol "Angels from the Realms of Glory" from "Les anges." The tune of the French song has been used with Montgomery's lyrics since then, but an 1867 melody by Henry Thomas Smart (1813-1879) is more commonly linked with the English carol today. In 1855 the carol was first published in France, and in 1862 the most familiar of several English translations, "Angels We Have Heard on High," was published without indication of authorship. The 1862 translation, though, varied considerably from the form now used. In 1916 an American carol collection printed the present version, again anonymous, and it is suspected that this was the first appearance of the revision.

Altogether, "Angels We Have Heard on High," with conjecture and anonymity strewn throughout its historical path, is probably the most historically fragile of all the international-class Christmas carols. Less is actually known about "Deck the Halls with Boughs of Holly," but there is little confusion or historical garbage associated with "Deck the Halls." There is even some doubt as to whether the song was from folk sources, as is commonly believed, or from mainstream sources. The use of Latin in the lyrics suggests creation in a church-affiliated environment and the high esthetic content and relative sophistication of the music imply substantial musical training. In any case, the song is one of the most beautiful and finely constructed pieces of the holiday season. Whether the excellent French lyrics or the similar-quality hybrid English translation is combined with the remarkable melodic blend of grace and subtle dynamism, "Angels We Have Heard on High" is artistically at the top of the carol genre. The highlight of the song, of course, is its buoyant, compelling, and highly elastic refrain which is quite conducive to singing or instrumentation. The noted English composer Martin Shaw (1875-1958) is just one of the talented persons who may have been lured by the attractiveness of the refrain. Shaw, possibly influenced by the famous piece, created a widely used "Gloria in excelsis Deo" choral composition entitled "Fanfare."

In all, "Angels We Have Heard on High" is one of the most tasteful, enduring, and appreciated of our carols. The essence of the piece is very aptly summarized in its Latin refrain "Gloria in excelsis Deo," or in English, "Glory to God in the highest."

# Hark! The Herald Angels Sing

Composite artistry occurs more than occasionally in the history of carols. Even the great carols can be the product of many hands. A classic example of such a musical stew is "Hark! The Herald Angels Sing." No fewer than five persons had direct and significant roles in the development of this Christmas pastiche of the first rank.

The carol was one of almost 9,000 poems written by the highly influential preacher and cofounder of Methodism, Charles Wesley (1707-1788). Other hymns from the facile pen of the talented hymnist include "Jesus, Lover of My Soul," "Ye Servants of God, Your Master Proclaim," "Love Divine, All Loves Excelling," "O for a Thousand Tongues to Sing," and "Christ the Lord Is Risen Today." Inspired by the joyous sounds of London church bells heard during a walk to church on Christmas Day, Wesley first published "Hark!" in a 1739 hymn collection issued by his equally famous brother John (1703-1791). In its original version, however, it was markedly different from what we are familiar with now. Even its title, "Hark How All the Welkin Rings," varied drastically from the ultimate form. ("Welkin," for your information, means "sky" or "heaven.") In 1753 George Whitefield (1714-1770), an eloquent preacher and close associate of the Wesleys in the Methodist movement, published a revision of the first two lines. Seven years later, in 1760, Reverend Martin Madan (1726-1790) revised lines seven and eight. With these major alterations, plus some minor adjustments, Wesley's eccentric "Welkin" poem became transformed into an uncommonly fine Christmas hymn.

It took three eighteenth-century poets to produce the lyrics of "Hark! The Herald Angels Sing." Similarly, two nineteenth-century musicians were required to supply a suitable tune. During the eighteenth century, and for about the first half of the nineteenth, the carol was only moderately popular because it was not set to an appropriate melody. The first tune used with "Hark!" was probably the superb one commonly affixed to Wesley's celebrated Easter song, "Christ the Lord Is Risen Today." But this piece of music was ill-fitting with the words of "Hark!," as were other melodies that were tried. In 1855, William Hayman Cummings (1831-1915), an English organist, adapted Welsey's hymn to some music by the brilliant German classical master Felix Mendelssohn (1809-1847). Cummings, reputedly a Mendelssohn enthusiast, discovered the melody in a relatively unknown June 1840 choral work entitled "Festgesang" ("Festival Song"). The composition was a special occasion piece created to honor the four hundredth anniversary of Gutenberg's invention of printing from movable type. Most of that work has fallen into obscurity, but the second chorus, "Gott ist Licht," ("God is Light"), has become a bit famous by being the source of the tune for "Hark!"

The synthesized carol was published in 1856 and again in 1857, and it was well on its way to international fame. Since then it has become an exceedingly popular and deeply appreciated Christmas song, one of the true elite of the holiday season. Yet it is also one of the strangest of carols. It is, in fact, the most peculiar piece from the top musical echelon of Christmas. In addition to its singular history which necessitated five major contributors, it is artistically odd, as well. The superlative tune, among the very best associated with any Christmas song, is actually an uncarol-like military-type march. While most carols fall into one of three types—the jolly Yuletide song, the tranquil nativity hymn, or the stately religious processional—"Hark!" is in contrast a rousing, fast-paced, dynamic, unhesitating, unpausing, breathtaking march in 4/4 time. Its bold, stirring, powerful, rapidly cadenced strides vigorously transport the singer or listener on a confident wave of martial music which loudly and joyfully proclaims the story of Christ's birth. Ironically, in this unconventional unbroken stream of assertive melody, in its breaking away from the common patterns of Christmas music, lies the very secret of the carol's immense popularity.

Even more idiosyncratic than Mendelssohn's music are Wesley's lyrics. They have been called a "masterpiece of condensed theology." That is, they are literally saturated with religious doctrine. Almost every phrase comprises a sermon. The first verse by itself presents us with almost the entire message of Christmas. Notwithstanding this overdose of theology, much of the poetry is good, especially verse one and the refrain which provide much emotional excitement and a strong infusion of esthetic excellence. The lyrics, in addition, are most compatible with the melody in rhythm and in tone, and the combination has resulted in a colossus among carols. And this is the most crucial consideration, for although we cannot ignore the carol's peculiarities and limitations, its fundamental reasons for existence are not to serve the purposes of the critic or analyst but to be sung, to be enjoyed, and to inspire. All three of these aspirations, certainly, are fully and continually achieved, season after season after season.

# It Came upon the Midnight Clear

No movie scenarist could have devised a more romantic setting for the composition of a Christmas poem. Reportedly, it was a cold winter day in December 1849. Outside, a snowfall was in progress, and inside, the fireplace in the study was erupting with warmth and light. No doubt this picturesque New England scene and the holiday season inspired the frail minister, and his pen scratched out several stanzas of verse about the birth of Jesus. They told of the singing of angels and the good news announcement brought to earth, and eloquently and flowingly expressed an unfaltering hope for the spiritual prosperity of all. The inspired lines were to become the literary half of one of the most renowned carols of all time, the classic standard "It Came upon the Midnight Clear."

Created in the atmosphere reminiscent of Hollywood productions, the poem was not the first Christmas poetry by the Reverend Edmund Hamilton Sears (1810-1876). In 1834, someplace in Massachusetts, he produced another Nativity lyric, the fairly well-known carol "Calm on the Listening Ear of Night." He also wrote several books on religious topics, was an editor for the Boston-based *Monthly Religious Magazine* from 1859 to 1871, and had a successful ministerial career. His longest pastorate was the Unitarian Church in rural Wayland, Massachusetts, where he stayed from 1848 to around 1865. Wayland was the locale for the idyllic and poetic environment which apparently helped precipitate the creation of his great 1849 Christmas hymn.

Sears' poem was published on December 29, 1849 in the *Christian Register*. One year later, in 1850, a tune by Richard Storrs Willis (1819-1900), set to the hymn "See Israel's Gentle Shepherd Stand," was published under the title "Study No. 23" in his *Church Chorals and Choir Studies*. Soon after, possibly that same year, the tune was rearranged to fit Sears' poetry. The rearrangement was probably by Willis himself but some sources state that Uzziah

Christopher Burnap (1834-1900) was responsible. If Burnap was the rearranger, he would have made his contribution at a young age. It is known for sure that no later than 1860 the tune was adapted by Willis to accommodate the lyrics of "While Shepherds Watched Their Flocks," and that the tune is also used with Sears' other carol, "Calm on the Listening Ear of Night."

These multiple usages of Willis' tune imply artistic merit far above the ordinary. Even its tune name, "Carol," suggests it very capably fulfills its mission as an exponent of the spirit of Christmas. Not only is it beautiful, readily accessible, and easily remembered, it has a slow, sort of rolling rhythm and a peaceful yet confident personality which has engendered the ingenuous but very apt description "carol-like." It is indeed unfortunate that although Willis' melody approaches in style and quality the ideal of a carol, and although it is among the more appreciated of holiday pieces, Willis never again duplicated the inspiration of his 1850 contribution to Christmas. Born to a prominent family in Boston, Willis studied music in Germany, developed a friendship with the great composer Felix Mendelssohn, was a very successful journalist, published several books and collections of music, and created a widely used arrangement of the popular hymn "Fairest Lord Jesus." Yet the little "Study No. 23," composed while he was pursuing his journalistic career in New York City, was to be his sole notable legacy to posterity.

Willis' lovely melody blends very sympathetically with Sears' outstanding lyrics, which contain a still-relevant social message of optimism, pacifism, goodwill, and the universal communality of humanity. These artistic assets brought to "Midnight Clear" the distinction of being the first great American Christmas carol. Furthermore, the song was apparently the forerunner of or the inspiration for an unusually productive generation of carol creation in the United States. In 1857 "We Three Kings of Orient Are" and "Jingle Bells" were produced. Probably a little later came "Up on the Housetop." In 1863 came the lyrics for "I Heard the Bells on Christmas Day." And in 1868 came "O Little Town of Bethlehem," the only American carol to exceed "It Came upon the Midnight Clear" in overall international acceptance. The two-decade period from 1849 to 1868 was, in its minor way, quite an extraordinary phenomenon in American cultural history.

# Susani

It would be easy to be confused about the carol "Susani." This attractive, upbeat, fourteenth-century German folk song has title similarities with two other Christmas pieces. Its variant title, "Vom Himmel hoch, O Englein kommt!" is close enough to Martin Luther's famous carol "Vom Himmel hoch, da komm ich her" to cause confusion. And the English titles of both songs reinforce the potential mix-up. The folk song has translations such as "From Heaven High, the Angels Came" and "From Heaven Above, O Angels Draw Nigh" while Luther's song has translations such as "From Heaven High I Come to You" and "From Heaven Above to Earth I Come."

As if this were not enough, "Susani" is even more closely affiliated in name with the fifteenth-century English folk carol "Susanni" or "A Little Child There Is Ybore." Another of the variant titles of the German song is "Susanni" (double n) which is exactly identical with its colleague from the British Isles. To complete the cycle of confusion, both "Susanni"'s use the same delightful German folk tune. Apparently, the English were so taken with the German song that they developed their own domestic version about a century later.

# THE SHEPHERDS

## Angels and Shepherds

Some carols defy precise theme classification. "Angels and Shepherds" (originally "Nesem vám noviny"), a seventeenth- or eighteenth-century folk song from Czechoslovakia, is one of these songs that is difficult to categorize exactly. It contains to some degree all the basic elements of the Christmas story, that is, the Nativity, angels, shepherds, the star, and the wise men. The eclectic nature of the song's lyrics is reflected in the diversity of the English translations, which include, in addition to "Angels and Shepherds," "Come All Ye Shepherds," "From Bethl'em's City," and "Hear What Great News We Bring." The most dominant theme, though, is the story of the shepherds. This is illustrated in the title of a well-known German version by Karl Riedel (1827-1888), who lived in the Bohemia region of Czechoslovakia. Riedel's song, which uses the same excellent melody, is entitled "Kommet, ihr Hirten" ("Come, You Shepherds").

Another famous carol has a situation similar to "Angels and Shepherds." The renowned sixteenth-century English folk song, "The First Nowell," also describes the spectrum of the Christmas story but has the most emphasis on the shepherds. And the similarity between the two carols does not end there. Both of them are contenders for the most famous carol created in their respective cultures. "Angels and Shepherds'" main competition is "Hajej, nynjej" ("Rocking"), an earlier folk song. But "Angels and Shepherds" is probably predominant because of its melody, which is one of the better pieces produced by the folk repertory.

# Come Leave Your Sheep

Over the centuries, shepherds have normally taken seriously their responsibilities for their helpless flocks. Why, then, should this carol exhort the tenders of sheep to abandon the animals under their care? Only an incident of great importance, in this case the birth of Jesus, could motivate the shepherds to such a course of action. Quite possibly, the poet who penned these verses understood the dilemma of the shepherds and consciously developed this subtle and creative approach to the story.

With lyrics created in the seventeenth or early eighteenth century and music from around 1875, "Quittez, pasteurs" is a fine French folk song perhaps originating in the Anjou region. In one sense the melody is possibly a century or two older, for the 1875 melody is actually an adaptation of an earlier folk air from the Besançon region of France. The older tune is also used with the carol. Though by no means an internationally renowned song, "Quittez, pasteurs" has received a moderate amount of attention as is demonstrated by at least six English translations which have been attached to it. "Come Leave Your Sheep" is a typical English version with other translations such as "O Come Away, Ye Shepherds," "O Leave Your Sheep," and "Leave, Shepherds, Leave" expressing similar compelling invitations to the simple shepherds.

# The First Nowell

"What's in a name? A carol by any other name will sound as sweet." This corruption of Shakespeare's legendary lines is probably valid for all Christmas carols, including the first-rank international folk favorite "The First Nowell." Yet although that carol's internal artistic integrity apparently is unaffected by a change of name, its external cultural visage is most certainly altered. Whenever the misguided and mistaken form "The First Noel" appears in the literature of carols, the usual and typical impression derived is that the carol is of French origin. But such an inference is thoroughly and unequivocally incorrect, for "The First Nowell" has absolutely no known connection with the land of "La Marseillaise" and Louis XIV.

"Nowell" is an English word dating back as far as the fourteenth century when Geoffrey Chaucer (ca. 1340-1400) used the term in his medieval masterpiece *The Canterbury Tales*. The English word is probably a derivative of an old French word, either "Noël" (Christmas) or "Nouvelle," (New) and the substitution of "Noël" thereby consistently results in a serious geographical misimpression. Still another French term, "naive," comes into the picture when characterizing the miscomprehension. If the song were really from France, it most likely would not have a partly English and partly French name but instead a completely French title such as "La première Noël."

All the historical evidence points clearly to the carol's being English, and probably from the remote Cornwall region in southwest England. Although the words were not published until 1823 and the tune not until 1833, a sixteenth-century date is reasonably certain. The song as we know it today, however, acquired a crucial alteration during the nineteenth century. When first published, part of the tune of the refrain was different. By the 1870s the notes for the words "Born is the King" had been changed, thus developing the version we are familiar with now. The person responsible for the inspired modification is unknown, but it is conceivable that Englishman John Stainer (1840-1901) could have been the rearranger. The revised form appeared in some important editions of carols issued by Stainer, the music editor, and text editor Ramsden Bramley (1833-1917). The idea for the alteration may have come from a tune set to lyrics similar to "The First Nowell"'s and which contained the same four-note pattern for "Born is the King" as the present version. The suspected melody was first published in William Wallace Fyfe's, *Christmas, Its Customs and Carols*, in 1860. If Stainer was the creator of the revision, as well as the joiner of "Greensleeves" with the lyrics for "What Child Is This?" as is conjectured, he must be regarded as a key contributor to two of the world's most important carols.

"The First Nowell" is perhaps the best-known carol of completely English origin, with only "God Rest You Merry, Gentlemen" also challenging for the title. But in spite of its great fame and popularity the song has been the recipient of a fair amount of negative criticism. The lyrics have been described as "crude poetry" and as "a sincere, devout attempt of a peasant to put the Christmas story into rhyme." In addition, the second verse erroneously refers to the shepherds, instead of the wise men, seeing the star, and that the star was "shining in the east," when it logically had to be in the western sky. Even the extremely appealing music has been similarly criticized. It has been described as "a terrible tune" and "repetitive to the point of hideous boredom." Apparently, part of the basis for such opinion is the belief that the tune may well have been based on a fragment from another song.

The critics of "The First Nowell," on the other hand, definitely exhibit an emotional dichotomy concerning the song. The same persons that cast such strong aspersions also have redeemed themselves with the following comments of praise, "so tuneful and full of joy and vigor," "beloved," and "will ever be a favorite because of its sincerity and simplicity." This is the dilemma of "The First Nowell." It is homely, unspectacular, and not highly esthetic. At the same time, it is comfortable, lovable, and enduring.

# Shepherd, Shake off Your Drowsy Sleep

Sleep is a common theme in carols. Usually the reference to slumber pertains to the infant Jesus, but there have been several Christmas songs which in some other context mention or imply a state of repose. These range from the 1599 classic "Wachet auf! Ruft uns die Stimme" ("Wake, Awake, for Night Is Flying") by Philipp Nicolai to the good seventeenth- or eighteenth-century French folk song "Haut, Haut, Peyrot" ("Wake Up, Pierre, Awaken"), to Irving Gordon's 1953 popular novelty "Too Fat for the Chimney," which begins with the line "Wake Up, Wake Up, Mommy Dear."

One of the best such carols is the seventeenth-century folk song from the Besançon area in eastern France, "Berger, secoue ton sommeil profound!" or "Chantons, bergers noël, noël." Its anonymous English translation is "Shepherd, Shake off Your Drowsy Sleep," with a variant which pluralizes shepherd. This intriguing title has perhaps promoted the fortunes of the carol as has most likely a popular arrangement of the tune by the English composer John Stainer (1840-1901). To be connected with Stainer would be a boost to any Christmas song, for he was the music editor for the 1871 collection, *Christmas Carols, New and Old*, in collaboration with text editor Henry Ramsden Bramley (1833-1917). That work was the first major English-language carol collection, and did much to publicize carols of all types. Accordingly, Bramley and Stainer rank among the leading propagators of the carol genre. They are exceeded in fame as collectors of carols in the English language only by the legendary personages Davies Gilbert (1767-1839) and William Sandys (1792-1874) whose much smaller 1822 and 1833 compilations pioneered the nineteenth-century carol-collecting movement.

# Shepherd's Carol

The first century and a half of the American colonies was not especially productive for Christmas music. Probably it was not until the second half of the eighteenth century that black spiritual carols came into existence, and mainstream carol writing did not flourish until the end of that century. Perhaps the first American carol composer of significance was the pioneering musician William Billings (1746-1800), a Boston-born hymn composer. In 1786 Billings published a lively and flowing song entitled "Shepherd's Carol" in his collection, *The Suffolk Harmony.*

Possibly partly due to its antiquated language such as the opening line, "Methinks I See a Heavenly Host," "Shepherd's Carol" is not very well known today. Yet its melody is quite approachable in style and also superior in quality, particularly in light of Billing's limited musical education. Arguably, the song is the oldest American carol still performed to any significant degree in the late twentieth century.

Two more generations passed before another notable Christmas piece (the music for "Joy to the World!") appeared on the American scene in 1839. Ironically, that very famous tune was not recognized as being American until much later. In effect, then, "Shepherd's Song," with its blend of quaintness and delightfulness, preceded by almost two-thirds of a century the renaissance of American carol writing which commenced in 1849 with "It Came upon the Midnight Clear."

# Whence Is That Goodly Fragrance

What possible connection can there be between the harsh brutality of Mack the Knife and a tender French folk carol about shepherds? As improbable as it may seem, there is a direct link between these two very contrasting themes. The common ground for both is John Gay's 1728 work, *The Beggar's Opera*. In 1928, German lyricist Bertolt Brecht (1898-1956) and German composer Kurt Weill (1900-1950) collaborated on the highly popular *Threepenny Opera* (originally *Die Dreigroschenoper*), which was based on *The Beggar's Opera* and which featured the knife-wielding Mack. In the original eighteenth-century work, Gay wrote words to go with popular melodies of the period. One of the pieces of music he included in the opera was the tune for the French folk carol "Quelle est cette odeur agréable?" Since so much connected with Gay's famous production is at least somewhat strange, no surprise should be forthcoming with the knowledge that the quiet carol was used as, of all things, a drinking song.

This gentle gem with softly rolling music and the very unusual mention of perfume was created in or around the seventeenth century, perhaps in the Lorraine region of northeast France. It is not especially well known outside of France, possibly because of its shy and unpretentious nature. Yet it is sufficiently popular to have received several English versions including "Whence Is That Goodly Fragrance," "What Is This Perfume So Appealing?," "What Is This Fragrance?," and "What Perfume This? O Shepherds Say!" And it has been accorded an additional degree of appreciation by being recorded by one of the world's most outstanding vocal groups, the Mormon Tabernacle Choir.

# While by My Sheep

American Theodore Baker (1851-1934) was a truly outstanding music scholar. He is best remembered for his famous multi-edition reference work, *Baker's Biographical Dictionary of Musicians*. He is also somewhat remembered for his exceptional skill at producing fine translations of carols, for he crafted the leading English lyrics for not just one, but three, carols of importance. And these three carols all deal with phenomena which are not part of the Christmas story, that is, bagpipes, echoes, and roses. The bagpipes were in the title of "Carol of the Bagpipers" ("Canzone d'i Zampognari"), echoes were the musical impression in "While by My Sheep" ("Als Ich bei meiner Schafen wacht"), and a rose was the allegory in "Lo, How a Rose E'er Blooming" ("Es ist ein Ros' entsprungen").

The echoing device in "While by My Sheep" is so effective that one of the variant titles of Baker's translation is "Echo Carol." That title was also employed by another translator who similarly appreciated the vividness of the echo simulation. Yet the song should not just be regarded a gimmick piece, for this sixteenth-century German folk carol is overall a very esthetic composition. It is one of the more superb members of a class of carols which must be categorized as being of the second level. In this case, second level refers to its degree of international recognition and not its artistic quality. If judged solely on its musical merit, it would surpass some of the first level or international class carols.

# While Shepherds Watched Their Flocks

The great English classical composer George Frederick Handel (1685-1759) has been commonly linked with two great English Christmas carols. One of these connections, as composer of the melody for "Joy to the World!," is completely bogus. The other connection, as composer of one of the melodies for "While Shepherds Watched Their Flocks," is, on the other hand, definitely valid. Handel's tune, which was adapted from his 1728 opera, *Siroë, King of Persia*, is worldwide perhaps the most popular of a number of melodies which have been affixed to the carol's lyrics. In America, the 1728 tune is clearly the most used.

The leading rival to Handel's lush and lively music is an anonymous sixteenth-century English tune called "Winchester Old." It was first published in Thomas Este's *The Whole Book of Psalms* (1592). The composer may well have been either Este (ca. 1540-1608) or George Kirbye (ca. 1560-1634) who is credited with the arrangement printed in the 1592 publication. No matter what the identity of the composer, the artistic result is a very creditable hymn tune that is quite compatible with the lyrics. But it took almost three hundred years for somebody to discover the harmony of the words and the 1592 music, for as far as is known the two partners were not joined until they appeared in the 1861 collection, *Hymns Ancient and Modern*.

The list of tunes for "While Shepherds Watched" is hardly limited to these two. Another occasionally used tune is the exceptional one composed by American Richard Storrs Willis (1819-1900) and attached to the lyrics of two other carols, "It Came upon the Midnight Clear" and "Calm on the Listening Ear of Night." Among the several lesser-used melodies are a United States folk tune and a tune by English composer and long-time parish clerk, William Knapp (1698-1768). The multiplicity of melodies, however, does not mean that the carol is without any dominant music, for Handel's tune and to a lesser extent the 1592 tune clearly predominate over the crowded field of suitors.

With three fine melodies as well as others matched with the lyrics, it would be easy to presume that the poetry is equally worthwhile. Such a presumption would be accurate, for the lyrics by Irish-born Nahum Tate (1652-1715), paraphrased from Luke 2:8-14, rate among the better carol texts in the English language. Indicative of Tate's talents as an author is his being named poet laureate of England in 1692. That was eight years before he published "While Shepherds Watched" in 1700 as part of the first supplement to the highly successful and long-enduring work, *The New Version of the Psalms of David*. The earlier publication was produced in collaboration with Nicolaus Brady in 1696.

Two further honors for Tate were his appointment as royal historiographer in 1702 and the lasting success of his version of *King Lear*, which had a happy ending. Tate's *King Lear* was reportedly more popular than Shakespeare's tragedy for about a century and a half. One has to appreciate anybody who can even temporarily surpass the literary efforts of the world's greatest dramatist. And one has to appreciate a carol which has strongly survived despite having neither a specific tune composed for it nor a clear monogamous tune relationship.

# THE "THREE KINGS"

## As with Gladness Men of Old

Very few famous carols have been written on the biblical theme of the Wise Men who journeyed from afar, followed a beckoning star, discovered the infant Jesus, and presented gifts to him. Only one famous carol, furthermore, avoids the common misconception that these men were necessarily kings or magi, or that they were three in number. The sole survivor of the "three king" myth is the popular nineteenth-century song "As with Gladness Men of Old."

On January 6, 1859, twenty-one-year-old William Chatterton Dix (1837-1898) of Bristol, England, was ill. During his stay in bed, he read the scripture lesson for the day, which was the Epiphany story of the Wise Men in Matthew 2:1-12. The passage sparked his imagination and his poetic propensities, and before long he had created the well-known carol. His artistic endeavors did not end there, for he also penned the verses for "What Child Is This?" around 1865 and for "Like Silver Lamps in a Distant Shrine" in 1871. In between poems, he earned his living as an insurance executive.

Two years later, William Henry Monk (1823-1889) adapted a tune to Dix's lyrics and published the combination in the 1861 English collection, *Hymns Ancient and Modern*. The tune originally was published in an 1838 German collection edited by Conrad Kocher (1786-1872). The authorship of the melody, which was written for the chorale "Treuer Heiland," is uncertain, but Kocher himself was most likely the composer. Reportedly, Dix did not like the tune, which ironically acquired the name "Dix." Yet in spite of Dix's opinion, and other tunes attempted as substitutes, Kocher's melody is used almost exclusively. Its fine esthetics and high public acceptance can also be inferred from its successful transfer to another well-known hymn, "For the Beauty of the Earth." A tune which is a standard setting for two top hymns must be regarded as a real winner.

# I Saw Three Ships

Legends about mysterious ships have developed throughout the long existence of mankind. The two most familiar such tales perhaps are the dreary tragedy of the Flying Dutchman destined to sail the seas until Judgment Day, and the happy, mindless image of three ships sailing into landlocked Bethlehem. This latter legend has been traced back to the twelfth century, specifically 1162, when three ships reputedly brought the relics of the Wise Men to Cologne, Germany. From this story evolved the English folk carol "I Saw Three Ships," which is by best guess from the fifteenth century.

Originally the three ships were intended as an allegory for the Wise Men, who supposedly number three, but with the passage of time another trio, the Holy Family, tended to displace the Wise Men. With either interpretation, the carol does not make a lot of sense. Yet it is a lively and likable concoction that has bouncily traversed five centuries of evolving cultural tastes, including a side trip through the folkways of eighteenth- or nineteenth-century Virginia where a derivative carol of the same name developed. Like so many other Christmas songs, analysis must be ignored, and idiosyncrasies overlooked so that we can enjoy the fun of singing this pleasurable piece on Christmas Day in the morning or any other time.

# The March of the Kings

If there were a category called "remarkable carols," "The March of the Kings" would be toward the top of the list. This delightful distinction has been gained, in addition, by not just one exceptional trait but by multiple factors. Not only is the melody truly and unequivocally first class, a vigorous and dynamic morsel of music, but the modern-sounding tune is all the more amazing because it was created in the thirteenth century, or about seven hundred years ago! To complete this trilogy of notable characteristics, it appears that both words and music have survived all these centuries without any appreciable alteration. No doubt a major contributor to its remaining intact for such a long time was the recognition that this carol was too superlative to be improved by tinkering or revision.

The birthplace of this rousing folk song was the Provence region of southern France, which, like "The March of the Kings," is toward the top of a list. The category in which Provence does so well could be designated "fertile locations for the creation of carols." (Also at the top on this list would be the Catalonia region of Spain and the West Country of England.) The original title, presumably, was "La marche des rois," although "Marche de Turenne" ("March of Turenne") is also used.

Notwithstanding its being the prime element in a famous carol, the tune is perhaps better known in another environment. In 1872 the celebrated French composer Georges Bizet (1838-1875) integrated an arrangement of the melody into his incidental music for the play, L'Arlésienne. It is in this context that so many persons have become familiar with the great melody. The carol function of the tune is not as widely recognized, in part because of the identification with Bizet, in part because the strong tune is not a typical carol melody, and in part because even the best English translations cannot overcome the antique feeling of the seven-centuries-old lyrics. Perhaps the song has too much age to be widely appreciated now. Perhaps, as good as it is, it is too far removed culturally to make a big impact on our contemporary society. It is, after all, the oldest well-known carol to have reached us in more or less its original form, and furthermore is one of the very oldest intact songs of any type, in any language, and from any culture.

# We Three Kings of Orient Are

It was all the fault of the gold, frankincense, and myrrh. From that brief mention of the gifts presented by the Wise Men to the child Jesus, as related in Matthew 2:11, evolved a very persistent and pervasive bit of religious folklore. The fine and expensive gifts, in the logic of the myth, meant that the visitors had to be of very high station, such as kings. The same logic pattern determined that the three types of offering had to correspond with the number of persons involved. Accordingly the erroneous but basically harmless illusion of "the Three Kings" has become a deeply embedded imperfection of our annual observance of Christmas.

The strong perpetuation of the myth by "We Three Kings of Orient Are," the best-known carol on the theme of the Wise Men, has done absolutely nothing to help the situation. But Pittsburgh-born John Henry Hopkins, Jr., (1820-1891) probably did not at all reflect on the theological implications of his little song when he wrote both words and music in 1857. At the time the versatile clergy-man, author, journalist, book illustrator, and designer of stained glass windows and other ecclesiastical objects, and was working as editor of the *Church Journal* in New York City. His only apparent purpose was to devise a special Christmas present for his beloved nephews and nieces. Annually, Hopkins made a holiday trip to the Burlington area of Vermont, which was the home of his father John Henry Hopkins, Sr., (1792-1868), the long-time Episcopal bishop of that state. As usual, bachelor Uncle Henry did not disappoint the children, for the dramatization of the story from Matthew was reportedly a big hit in the Hopkins household.

The success of "We Three Kings" within the author's family circle was soon replicated in the outside world. As early as 1859, the song may have been put into print. Although the 1859 date is uncertain, by 1865 it had definitely appeared in the literature two times, first in Hopkins' 1863 collection, *Carols, Hymns, and Songs*, and subsequently in a separately published, specially illustrated 1865 version. Both the 1863 and 1865 publications carried the variant title "Three Kings of Orient." This rapid sequence of publication no doubt reflected the quickly spreading fame of Hopkins' carol, which ultimately became one of the most famous of all Christmas pieces. Because of this enduring musical amusement, and to a lesser extent another notable carol, "Gather Around the Christmas Tree," Hopkins has received a microniche in history and the appellation "Vermont's Father Christmas." Such a dubbing is geographically inappropriate, for Hopkins neither was born in that state nor did he create his carol there.

In spite of the unbiblical aspects of Hopkins' lyrics, and some negative criticism and even exclusion from hymnals because of the inaccuracies, "We Three Kings" is a perennial favorite. But why this is so is a bit of a puzzle. The lyrics are clearly inferior, as is graphically exemplified in the very first lines, "We three kings of Orient are, Bearing gifts we traverse afar." These (and other lines) are grammatically questionable and clumsy in poetic flow. There is actually a pause after the word are, reinforced by a rest notation in the music. Another particularly awkward section is "Frankincense to offer have I, Incense owns a Deity nigh." The refrain, on the other hand, is reasonably good.

The melody is, fortunately, far more esthetic than the words. Although not a truly outstanding tune, it is attractive and accessible, smooth and rhythmic, and has an appropriate coating of mysticism and oriental flavoring. Additionally, it imparts the sensation of continuous motion analogous to the long journey of the Wise Men. Putting aside the various little problems associated with "We Three Kings," a view of the carol as a composite entity brings forth the conclusion that the song is overall a very effective piece. Despite its artistic and theological deficiencies, it has fulfilled its mission to relate the story from Matthew better than any other work of music ever has.

# THE NIGHTS OF CHRISTMAS

## Brightest and Best

The slums of London are not the most promising territory for the development of a carol tune. Yet it was at the Gifford Hall Mission in the Islington section of the British capital that James Procktor Harding (1850-1911) first presented the anthem from which his tune for the carol "Brightest and Best" would be derived. The June 1892 composition by the long-time civil service clerk, church organist, and amateur musician is only one of the nearly 20 settings for the carol's lyrics, but it is probably the best known. Some of the variety of musical alternatives are a melody by J. F. Thrupp (1827-1867), a United States folk air, and a seventeenth-century German tune.

The sole constant factor in the carol is the image-filled poetry by Reginald Heber (1783-1826). Published in 1811, the words are also entitled "Brightest and Best of the Sons of the Morning" and "Star of the East." The latter title is based on one of the lines of the first verse, which is a romanticized representation of the star of Bethlehem. The latter title has also caused some mix-up with the folk carol "Star in the East," a Southern States song which may well have been based on Heber's poem and which shares a folk tune with its probable English relative. This title also could be confused with the unrelated 1890 Christmas song "Star of the East" by Americans George Cooper and Amanda Kennedy.

In contrast to the shining visage and exuberant tone of the title, Heber's lyrics, although quite good, are neither the brightest and best of English carols nor of its author's hymnodical output. Heber, an Oxford-educated Anglican cleric, also wrote the superb and extremely popular hymn "Holy, Holy, Holy!" Both this master-piece and "Brightest and Best" were produced during Heber's 1807-1823 tenure as vicar at the small village of Hodnet in Shropshire. After his artistically productive stay in this remote location in western England, Heber moved to an even more remote setting. From 1823 to his untimely death in 1826, he was bishop of Calcutta, India, which has also been noted for its share of slums.

# Carol of the Bagpipers

Italy's fine musical heritage is almost legendary. Great composers such as Claudio Monteverdi, Antonio Vivaldi, Domenico Scarlatti, Gioacchino Rossini, Giusseppe Verdi, and Giacomo Puccini, famous opera houses such as La Scala in Milan, and a rich folk tradition all combine to make Italy one of the premier wellsprings of Western music. It is therefore more than a little surprising to discover that the contributions of that nation to the body of internationally known Christmas carols has been comparatively negligible. In fact, no song from Italy is among the worldwide carol elite.

The most famous carols entirely of Italian origin are probably "Dormi, Dormi, O Bel Bambin," a folk carol with several English translations ("Sleep, Sleep, Lovely Babe," "Sleep, O Sleep, My Lovely Child," and similar titles) and "Canzone d'i Zampognari," a folk carol known in English under the titles "Carol of the Bagpipers," "Bagpiper's Carol," "On That Most Blessed Night," and "Song of the Bagpipers." This latter song, which originated in Sicily in or around the seventeenth century, is almost surely the leading Italian carol. Its appealing lyrics, which refer to the night of Jesus' birth with the bright star shining in heaven, and its gentle and lilting melody harmoniously create a dual impression of serenity and joyfulness. One may not think of bagpipes and serenity as coexisting, or in fact associate the pipes with Italy, but in this song all these elements come together.

In the first half of the eighteenth century, the very attractive tune caught the attention of the great composer George Frederick Handel, possibly during Handel's 1708 travels in Italy. When one listens to Handel's 1742 choral work, *Messiah*, the melody can be found as the opening for "He shall feed his flock." Accordingly, there is a little masterpiece intruding so appropriately in the big masterpiece.

# How Brightly Beams the Morning Star

The year 1599 is very unusual in the annals of Christmas music. That is one of the few years in which two famous international carols were created or printed. Another is 1853 when both "Good Christian Men, Rejoice" and "Good King Wenceslas" were published. What separates 1599 from 1853 is that only the lyrics were new to 1853, while both words and music were original to 1599. Also, 1857 is noted for the coincidental birth of two great carols, "We Three Kings of Orient Are" and "Jingle Bells." What distinguishes 1599 from 1857 is that in the later year the carols were by two different composers, while in the earlier year they were by the same person.

The 1599 individual was Philipp Nicolai (1556-1608), a prominent German Lutheran pastor. He had positions in several cities including Hamburg (where he died). His most-remembered appointment, though, was at Unna in Westphalia where he created the words and music for "Wachet auf! Ruft uns die Stimme," and "Wie schön leuchtet der Morgenstern" (originally "Wie herlich strahlt der Morgenstern"). Both of these positive-outlook musical gems were created, amazingly, during a depressing period of pestilence when hundreds of lives were lost to bubonic plague at Unna. The strain of the scourge seemed to give a special spiritual urge to Nicolai, for his gift to posterity is entirely wrapped in this dual hymnodical package.

The lyrics for the "Wie schön leuchtet" portion of this parcel were partially redone in 1768 by Johann Adolf Schlegel (1721-1793), including the revision of the first line. They also have been re-wrapped into English a number of times. The best-known English versions are two separate translations, "O Morning Star, How Fair and Bright" and "How Brightly Beams the Morning Star," both by Englishwoman Catherine Winkworth (1827-1878). The music for this song, which may have been influenced by the fine fourteenth-century melody used for the carols "Joseph, lieber Joseph mein" ("Joseph, Dearest Joseph Mine"), and "Resonet in laudibus," is one of the better tunes from Germany. It has been utilized as an accompaniment for the carol "Die Könige" ("The Kings") by Peter Cornelius (1824-1874), and as the basis for Johann Sebastian Bach's Cantata No. 1 (1725). Bach's arrangement for the cantata is the version most commonly used today.

All of this attention to Nicolai's carol is indicative of its continuing popularity. It even has been the recipient of a highly laudatory epithet, "Queen of the chorales," implying a rank second only to the "King," which just happens to be Nicolai's other carol, "Wachet auf!" In other words, Nicolai was the father of talented and famous royal twins.

# O Holy Night

In every way, the brilliant and polished French carol "Cantique de Noël" appears to be without blemish or defect. The religious lyrics are excellent, the melody is superb, and the mood exuding from the pair in performance has few peers. In public acceptance, too, the song ranks extremely high. It is the most famous carol from France and belongs to the top echelon of carols on an international basis. Why, then, would anybody want to ban or censor this esthetic and inoffensive masterpiece of the Christmas season? The answer lies not in the characteristics of the carol itself, but in some persons' perceptions of the backgrounds of its creators. The story begins in 1847. In the Rhône Valley of France, noted for its fine wines, distinctive Provençal culture, and colorful history, there lived a man whose existence touched upon all three of these regional characteristics. Placide Cappeau (1808-1877), a lifelong resident of the small community of Roquemaure, a few miles north of the historic city of Avignon, was by profession a commissionaire of wines, by avocation an occasional writer of verse in both French and the regional dialect Langue d'oc, and by pure luck a minor figure in history. The fortunate sequence of events began when Cappeau became friends with a Parisian couple named Laurey. The Laureys had temporarily relocated to southern France so that Monsieur Laurey could follow his civil engineering career by building a bridge across the Rhône River near Roquemaure. Just before Cappeau left for Paris on a business trip, the parish priest asked the part-time poet to write a Christmas poem and to take it to the famous Parisian composer Adolphe Adam (1803-1856) for a musical setting. Adam was an acquaintance of Madame Laurey, who was a singer. Reportedly, on December 3, 1847, about halfway on the long coach ride to Paris, Cappeau received the inspiration for the poem "Minuit, Chrétiens."

Cappeau was a total obscurity when he contacted Adam in Paris. The composer, in contrast, was at the peak of his fame at that time.

A highly popular and prolific musician, Adam had only a few years before, in 1841, produced his salient masterwork, the ballet *Giselle*. The most important ballet prior to the 1870 landmark dance classic *Coppélia*, which was composed by Adam's protege, Léo Delibes (1836-1891), *Giselle* is called the *Hamlet* of ballet because of its tragic story, its challenge for ballerinas, and its exceptionally esthetic duo of choreography and music. *Giselle*, still one of the very top ballets today, was the most famous work by Adam. The little melody he was to create for Madame Laurey's friend was to become the clear occupant of the second place in Adam's reputation.

After Cappeau brought his lines to Adam, the facile musician took only a few days to complete the carol. The premiere performance of the song was, as intended, at the midnight mass in the church of Roquemaure on Christmas 1847. It is quite conceivable that the unsuspecting audience was delightfully stunned by the soulful beauty of the partially homegrown song. Despite this remote and unheralded beginning, the song, within a generation or so, became one of the classics of the Christmas season. Perhaps first published around 1855 in an organ arrangement by Schott and Company in London, the carol ultimately received various musical treatments and was translated into many languages. The best-known English version, "O Holy Night," was by the American music critic and journalist John Sullivan Dwight (1818-1893).

It is because the carol is so famous and popular that it has been especially targeted by some persons as an undesirable element of Christmas. The real reason for the attacks is not artistry but the alleged negative characteristics of the carol's creators. Adam was from a non-Christian background and additionally was predominantly a theatrical composer of light operatic works and ballets, an arena far removed from the theological scene. Even worse, Cappeau has been described as a social radical, a freethinker, a socialist, and a non-Christian. In part, this categorization is true. Late in his life he adopted some of the more "extreme" political and social views of his era, such as opposition to inequality, slavery, injustice, and all kinds of oppression. These attitudes were clearly indicated in an 1876 poem, "Le Château de Roquemaure," a 4,000-line philosophical poetical flop in which Cappeau repudiated his 1847 lyrics and drastically revised their content and outlook. The controversial

views, though, were confined only to his last years which are
marked by obvious eccentricity. The strangest act of that period was
a request to be buried upright after his death. At the time he wrote
his sensitive and inspired verses, in contrast, he must have been
something of a conventional Christian or otherwise the parish priest
would not have requested a religious poem.

Overall, the impact of "Cantique de Noël" on Western society is
suggested by the following unsubstantiated anecdote. During the
Franco-Prussian War of 1870-1871, the French and Germans were
facing each other in trenches outside of Paris. On Christmas Eve, a
French soldier unexpectedly jumped out of his trench and sang
"Cantique de Noël." Awestruck by this surprise performance, the
Germans did not fire on the Frenchman and instead responded with
their own national Christmas institution, Martin Luther's "Vom
Himmel hoch" ("From Heaven Above to Earth I Come"). Whether
or not this incident is true or apocryphal, it ideally illustrates the
legacy of the carol. If it is history, it reflects the song's discernible
cultural impact. If it is folklore, it mirrors the carol's continuing and
pervasive influence on the human imagination.

# Silent Night

Throughout the history of civilization there has been an enor-
mously wide variety of phenomena which have directly or indirectly caused the creation of the landmarks of our culture. In the case of
the world's most famous Christmas song, "Silent Night," the indirect initiator of the events that produced this great carol, reportedly,
was none other than everyday, common, ordinary rust! (Those mis-
informed readers who insist on believing the cuter anecdote about
the chewing mouse and the organ bellows can go on to the next
essay.) Cynics can also depart who automatically reject the completely plausible details of the birth of this beloved carol simply
because there is no firm documentation for an event that occurred
almost 200 years ago involving obsure persons in a remote setting.

But the rest of the story of "Silent Night" is anything but common or ordinary. The time, Christmas Eve in 1818, was quite appropriate. The place, St. Nicholas' Church in Oberndorf, Upper
Austria, was admirably suited for a Christmas event, as its name
implies, and also for a musical happening. The church was only 11
miles from historic Salzburg, which was the birthplace of the incomparable Wolfgang Amadeus Mozart as well as the location of
the music festival won by the Von Trapp family singers in *The
Sound of Music*. The cast of characters, on the other hand, seems
very unlikely for the drama in which they participated. The first
member of the dubious entourage was Father Joseph Mohr
(1792-1848), the assistant priest at St. Nicholas. He was of illegiti-
mate parentage, had a chronic drinking problem, and was frequently transferred from parish to parish. Because the Salzach River
flowed close to the church, excess humidity had caused rust to
develop in the organ thus preventing it from being played. With a
musicless Christmas Eve looming immediately before him, Mohr
responded by jotting down a six-stanza poem beginning with the
words "Stille Nacht, heilige Nacht."

The second of the dramatis personae enters at this point. He was Franz Gruber (1787-1863), a schoolteacher who was supplementing his income (moonlighting) by playing the organ at St. Nicholas. The odd thing about Gruber is that he really should not have been at Oberndorf. In a nineteenth-century version of double moonlighting, he was supposed to be the organist at the church in nearby Arnsdorf, but for economic reasons he had a stepson act as his surrogate at Arnsdorf. After Mohr completed his hastily conceived verses, he brought them to Gruber for a musical setting. Within a few hours Gruber devised a simple tune arranged for two solo voices, chorus, and guitar. At the midnight service Mohr and Gruber sang their solution to the emergency, accompanied by the choir and Gruber on the guitar.

Except for the final star of the episode, "Stille Nacht, heilige Nacht" would have folded after its premiere. In the spring of the next year an organ repairman named Karl Mauracher, from Zillerthal, came to Oberndorf to fix the rusted instrument. Before he left he had secured a copy of the song, and after returning home began to spread the pleasant little carol throughout the Tyrol region. Soon the song was brought to more distant places by two traveling singing families, the Strassers and the Rainers. The Strassers, also from Zillerthal, performed the carol at the Leipzig fair in 1831 and before the King of Prussia in 1834, thus assuring its propagation throughout Germany. The Rainers, traveling even farther, traversed the ocean and presented the song to the populace of New York City in 1839. For two decades, the carol passed orally from person to person in typical folk song fashion. It was not until 1838 that "Stille Nacht" was first published in a collection called *Leipziger Gesangbuch*.

Partly because of this folkish method of transmission, and partly because there were no historical records relative to the song's creation, the carol for several decades was widely considered to be an anonymous Tyrolean folk piece. It was also thought to be an obscure work by one of the Austrian classical composers, particularly Johann Michael Haydn (1737-1806), the younger brother of the great Franz Joseph Haydn (1732-1809). Aided by information supplied by Gruber's son, a government investigation in 1854 determined the truth of the matter. By that time the carol had become world famous. Tragically, Mohr probably never knew that his carol had become a sensation although he lived for 30 years after his historic achievement.

Doubly ironic, at about the same time that rurally isolated Mohr died in ignorance of what he had done, the carol had made sufficient impact across the Atlantic for an English version, a free paraphrase, to be published in 1849. Not long after followed another English treatment, this time the dominant 1863 translation, "Silent Night." The three-stanza conversion by John Freeman Young (1820-1885), who later was to become the Episcopal bishop of Florida, is so well done and is so very familiar to us today that it is difficult to conceive anybody wanting to try another. Yet there have been at least three other English versions, all of which have failed to move the poetic mountain built by Young.

There is little doubt, if any, that "Silent Night" is the most popular carol in the world. There is also no doubt that there are at least several other Christmas songs which are intrinsically more artistic in content and more stimulating to the esthetic senses. Yet "Silent Night" finds more public acceptance than all the other carols in spite of being poetically and/or musically surpassed by some of its rivals. The factors which make it rise above the competition are intangible and perhaps for that reason debatable. One ingredient is its unextreme middle-of-the-road personality. "Silent Night" is, first of all, sort of a cross between folk simplicity and mainstream substantialness. In addition, it is devout in tone but not weighed down by theological trappings, and it is old enough to be firmly established in our culture without being archaic in the slightest. Another ingredient is its calming and soothing mood and style, or in other words, it makes us feel good. It does not stimulate, excite, or challenge, but instead acts to a fair degree as a holiday pacifier. Most of all, it has those indefinable qualities which make it "beloved." The highly romantic background of the carol's creation, which has similarities to the circumstances surrounding the 1868 carol "O Little Town of Bethlehem," no doubt contributes to this mass endearment. But possibly the main source of the widespread sentiment is the pervasive feeling that "Silent Night" embodies the spirit of the holiday more than any other musical piece ever created. It is, in that sense, the musical symbol of Christmas.

# Star of the East

New York City lyricist George Cooper (1840-1927) was associated with many composers during his long career. At the famous end of the spectrum, he was the closest friend of the renowned American composer Stephen Foster (1826-1864) during Foster's stay in New York. Due to excessive drinking and dire poverty, Foster lived in a hotel room in the Bowery, and it was there that his friend Cooper discovered him bleeding from an accident. Cooper took Foster to Bellevue Hospital where Foster died three days later.

At the obscure end of the spectrum, Cooper was the collaborator with little-known American composer Amanda Kennedy on the 1890 carol "Star of the East." This very good religious song retains a degree of popularity a century after its composition. It should not be confused with the better-known English carol "Brightest and Best," which is also called "Star of the East," or with the lesser-known American folk carol "Star in the East." Much of the reason for the carol's continuing prosperity is Kennedy's tune, the only thing for which she is remembered. Apparently, the star motif which brought Kennedy her thin slice of fame was a favorite with her, for somewhat earlier, in 1883, she published a piano piece "Star of the Sea." Cooper, too, had more than one artistic contact with the star theme. He was the lyricist with musician J.P. Skelly on a piece called "Twinkle, Twinkle Little Star," but unfortunately for them not the famous song of that name.

# There's a Song in the Air

"What I did on my summer vacation" is a stereotypical composition theme for school children returning in the fall. If this were asked of New Hampshire-born Karl P. Harrington (1861-1953) in the autumn of 1904, the reply could have been, "During my July vacation at North Woodstock, New Hampshire, I composed a carol tune which someday will be world famous!" Of course, it is highly doubtful that Harrington, a respected Latin professor, organist, and musicologist, said or thought any such thing, but it is fact that his 1904 tune soon came to the attention of the musical world.

Harrington was one of the music editors for the 1905 Methodist hymnal. He was dissatisfied with the tune which had been used with the poem "There's a Song in the Air" by Josiah Gilbert Holland (1819-1881). He created his tune as an alternative, and it was printed in the hymnal as the song's second tune, along with about a dozen other tunes by Harrington. Of all these melodies, only one emerged into any prominence. Harrington's variant became a very well-liked fixture to Holland's poetry, and the tune it replaced as well as the other pieces of music by Harrington were lost in the dust of time. Harrington's tune, furthermore, has eclipsed in popularity the several other melodies which have been attempted as substitutes in the carol.

The author of the excellent verse was born in Massachusetts and trained to be a physician. After practicing medicine for a while, he switched his career to literature and journalism. One of his major achievements was serving as editor of *Scribner's Magazine* from 1870 until his death, on top of collaborating in its establishment. While he was working at the New York magazine, he published the carol in his 1872 collection *The Marble Prophecy and Other Poems*. One of the better American carol lyrics, Holland's words are expressive and exuberant. The highly positive tone, emphasized by frequent use of exclamation points, is one of the strengths of the poem. Another of its assets is its skillful portrayal of the star of Bethlehem as exemplified in the second line "There's a star in the sky!" and most of all in the dynamic fifth line "And the star rains its fire while the beautiful sing."

# 'Twas in the Moon of Wintertime

Among the least likely locales for the genesis of the first carol in the Americas would be the Indian-occupied hinterlands of Ontario. Yet in the very early known history of that Canadian province, around 1641 or 1642, the French Jesuit missionary Jean de Brébeuf (1593-1649) created the words for the Huron-language Christmas song "Jesus ahatonhia." The carol, which was specifically written as a part of Brébeuf's mission to the Huron Indians, was set to the sixteenth-century French folk song "Une jeune pucelle."

After Father Brébeuf was killed by invading Iroquois Indians, the song fortunately was orally preserved by the Hurons, who were especially attached to the celebration of the birth of the Son of God. About a century after its composition, another Jesuit priest discovered the carol and put it down on paper. By doing this, the later priest not only saved this unusual carol from extinction, but also kept alive one of the more fascinating stories surrounding any carol. Most commonly known in English as J. E. Middleton's translation "'Twas in the Moon of Wintertime" or "The Huron Carol," Brébeuf's contribution to Canadian civilization is perhaps the leading carol of that superlative nation. Two other possible rivals are the folk songs "La guignolée" ("Carol of the Mistletoe Singers") and "D'où viens tu, bergére?" ("Whence Art Thou, My Maiden?"). This latter piece may not really be in the running, however, for although it has been attributed to Quebec, it most likely originated in France.

"'Twas in the Moon of Wintertime" is triply unique. Its role as the pioneering New World carol is one facet of this uniqueness, as is its being the only well-known carol constructed via the medium of an Indian language. The third singular trait is its picturesque moon theme, which is a rarity. These three characteristics have helped to ensure its continuance into the late twentieth century.

# Watchman, Tell Us of the Night

The Old Testament is not usually associated with Christmas carols since the biblical sources for the greatest holiday in Western civilization come from the New Testament. However, one famous carol, "Watchman, Tell Us of the Night," is based on a passage from an Old Testament prophet. In Isaiah 21:11-12 there is the intriguing inquiry "Watchman, what of the night?" upon which Englishman John Bowring (1792-1872) built his Advent hymn. Apparently he intended that the verses, which are arranged in question and answer format, portray the transition from night unto day not only in the literal chronological sense but also in a symbolic theological context. His poetry could be interpreted as an optimistic prediction that the darkness of evil will give way to the light of good under the impetus of the coming of the Son of God.

Bowring was one of the most interesting individuals ever affiliated with a carol. He was a world traveler and reportedly read 200 and spoke 100 languages. He was a friend of the influential philosopher Jeremy Bentham (1748-1832) and served as editor of Bentham's *Westminster Review*. He was a member of Parliament, minister plenipotentiary to China, governor of Hong Kong, and was knighted by Queen Victoria. While in Hong Kong, he even precipitated a minor war with China. He also was a prolific author, producing 36 volumes of writings. His most-remembered literary piece may be "Watchman," which was first printed in 1825.

Several musical settings have been devised for "Watchman." These include melodies by German composer Jakob Hintze (1622-1702), published in 1678 (there is some doubt as to authorship), by Welsh composer Joseph Parry (1841-1903), published in 1879, by English composer George Job Elvey (1816-1893), published in 1858, and by American composer Lowell Mason (1792-1872). The most-used settings seem to be the ones by Hintze, who was a Berlin court musician and music editor, and by Parry, who overcame dire family poverty and a childhood job in the puddling furnaces to rise to become a respected music professor and the composer of the first Welsh opera. Parry's tune is also used for Charles Wesley's famous hymn "Jesus, Lover of My Soul" (1738).

The international flavor of Bowring's activities undoubtedly contributed substantially to the enhancement of his life. In contrast, the international mix of tunes used with his carol probably has had a detrimental effect on the acceptance of the song. No single melody has particularly touched the popular fancy, and accordingly the carol has surely suffered to some degree. Although some of the melodies are quite good, too many tunes can spoil the carol.

# CHRISTMAS WORSHIP

# Break Forth, O Beauteous Heavenly Light

Most prominent poets and musicians over the centuries have avoided diverting their talents to the direct composition of Christmas carols. As a whole, carols are anonymous, or the most famous activity of an otherwise obscure person, or the incidental by-product of a famous person. In other words, carols are overall the domain of the obscure. There are some notable exceptions, for example, Martin Luther, Isaac Watts, Charles Wesley, Adolphe Adam, Benjamin Britten, and Irving Berlin.

The incomparable master Johann Sebastian Bach (1685-1750) is not one of the exceptions. Despite a prolific artistic output, Bach never directly composed a Christmas song. Yet his affiliation with the carol genre is more than casual or occasional. Among Bach's carol connections are: Isaac Watts' 1715 poem "Hush, My Dear, Lie Still and Slumber," which was attached to one of his tunes; Philipp Nicolai's famous 1599 carols "Wie schön leuchtet der Morgenstern" ("How Brightly Beams the Morning Star") and "Wachet auf! Ruft uns die Stimme" (Wake, Awake, for Night Is Flying") which were incorporated into two of his cantatas; and several well-known carols which were integrated into his famous 1734 Christmas Oratorio. Luther's carol, "Vom Himmel hoch, da komm ich her" ("From Heaven Above to Earth I Come") is the best known of these. "Brich an, du schones Morgenlicht," whose dominant translation "Break Forth, O Beauteous Heavenly Light," by Englishman John Troutbeck (1833-1889), is perhaps the second most famous.

Johann Rist (1607-1667), the author of the lyrics for "Brich an," was a physician and pastor in Wedel, Germany, near Hamburg. Although he wrote about 680 hymns and was honored as poet laureate in 1645 by Emperor Ferdinand III, his carol is essentially his only historical legacy. The same almost applies to Johann Schop (ca. 1590-ca. 1664), whose melody appeared with the text when it was published in Rist's 1641 *Himmlische Leider.* Schop, a close friend of Rist, was music editor for the 1641 collection as well as an accomplished performer on several varied instruments. What elevates Schop above the status of being remembered for just one work is the adaptation of another of Schop's tunes for Bach's renowned "Jesu, Joy of Man's Desiring." Bach's treatment of both of Schop's melodies are much better known than the originals, but there can be no doubt about the debts owed to Schop. The monumental figure Bach and the minor figure Schop are therefore linked together in a peculiar polarity of fame.

# The Garden of Jesus

The symbol of growing plants is a fairly common one in the carols of the late Middle Ages and Renaissance. Four Christmas folk songs of consequence from the fourteenth or fifteenth centuries contain allusions to botanical themes. These are the English carol "There Is No Rose of Such Virtue," the German carols "Es ist ein Ros' entsprungen" ("Lo, How a Rose E'er Blooming) and "Es stot ein Lind im Himmelrich" ("There Stood in Heaven a Linden Tree"), and the Dutch carol "Jesus' Bloemhof" or "Heer Jesus heeft een hofken."

Of fifteenth-century folk origins (probably first published in 1609), "Jesus' Bloemhof" is a fine and imaginative early worship carol. A good example of Dutch Christmas songs, and quite possibly the most popular carol from the Netherlands, it has been translated at least five times. The English versions include "The Garden of Jesus," "Lord Jesus Has a Garden," "King Jesus Hath a Garden," and "Our Master Hath a Garden," and all emphasize the flowers in the allegorical horticultural enterprise. How the flower imagery, which equates Jesus and several virtues to various botanical species, is related to Christmas could well be debated. What is more certain is that the carol is among the more esthetic carols of its era and that despite the quaintness of the garden concept to us today it is a song well worth preserving for future Christmas observances.

# Love Came Down at Christmas

As a whole, the success of the more popular Christmas carols is a direct reflection of the widespread public acceptance of its music. An exceptionally attractive melody can compensate for inferior lyrics, and even with good words the tune is typically the foundation of the carol's continued existence. This opposing scenario, though, rarely occurs. It is seldom that a carol's lyrics can overcome the disadvantages of not having a tune (or two or three) which has caught the imagination of holiday audiences.

One exception to this general pattern is the case of "Love Came Down at Christmas." This simple, direct, and sincere 1885 poem, the product of the outstanding English poet Christina Rossetti (1830-1894), has successfully survived in its role as a Christmas song in spite of its tunelessness. This is not to say that "Love Came Down" has never been linked to any melody. Rather, it is a way to describe the situation of multiple melodic associations without any clearly dominant combinations. Many carols have more than one melody, but usually at least one tune stands out in quality or popularity. Among the tunes which have been joined with "Love Came Down" are an eighteenth- or nineteenth-century Irish folk melody, and tunes by Sidney Hann, John Ernest Borland, Edgar Pettman, and Reginald O. Morris. None of these pieces of music or composers even approach being household words. In contrast, Rossetti's other famous carol, "In the Bleak Mid-Winter," has a single tune which despite its singular style sustains its literary mate quite strongly.

# O Come All Ye Faithful

King Philip II of Spain (1527-1598) was probably the most powerful ruler of the sixteenth century. He is remembered for a number
of negative actions, including the infamous and disastrous Armada
sent against England in 1588. Among his beneficial accomplishments was the establishment of a Roman Catholic college for Englishmen at Douai in northern France. The college became the
nucleus for a famous center from which two landmark cultural
events evolved during the following two centuries. In the seventeenth century the important Douay Version of the Old Testament
was developed. In the eighteenth century one of the greatest of all
Christmas carols, "Adeste Fideles," was created in the 1740s.

One of the Catholic Englishmen living in Douai at that time was
John Francis Wade (1711-1786). In addition to being a music teach-
er, Wade was also a music copyist (the eighteenth-century version
of a photocopier). So when Wade produced a four-stanza Latin
hymn entitled "Adeste Fideles" between the years 1740 and 1743,
it was commonly presumed that the song was simply copied by
Wade. But Wade was actually the creator of both words and music.
Yet a full two centuries passed before research published in 1947
conclusively proved his real role. In between, the carol was attributed to the Portuguese, Saint Bonaventura of Italy, the Germans,
and the Cistercian order of monks. Also, English organist John
Redding (d. 1692) has been named as the composer of the tune.

All of the above attributions have no relation to the true history
of the carol, except for the Portuguese who actually did play a major
part in the song's propagation. Sometime in the late eighteenth
century, Wade's carol was carried to England, most likely by returning English Catholics. By 1782 it was published in London. (The
lyrics alone had previously been printed in France in 1760.) In or
around 1797, the song was initiated in the chapel of the Portuguese
embassy in London, and soon the carol became very popular

throughout the country. About a half century later, its most successful English translation developed from the increasing groundswell
of the carol's impact. In 1841 a London Anglican clergyman, Frederick Oakeley (1802-1880), wrote a version beginning with the line
"Ye faithful, approach ye." Later on, after converting to Roman
Catholicism, he also converted his poem to a new form, "O come,
all ye faithful," and published it in London in 1852. Although
almost 50 other translations have been produced, Oakeley's 1852
poetry, in the very familiar three-stanza version commonly printed,
is probably used more than all the others combined.

In artistry and public acceptance, "O Come All Ye Faithful" has
very few peers. It is one of the best-loved and most-performed of
Christmas songs, arguably in the top five or so of holiday pieces.
Oakeley's translation is extremely well liked and even verses two
and three are widely remembered by singers throughout the world.
And the melody is exceptionally fine. It is an extraordinarily competent processional which is not surpassed by many other proces-
sionals of any musical genre. To some extent, it is vaguely reminiscent of the superlative fourth movement of Beethoven's Ninth
Symphony (the "Choral"). Perhaps it is heresy to presume that any
carol tune not written by a classical composer could possibly approach the quality of classical music, but Wade's melody (and a few
others) does at least come close.

A very appropriate epithet for "O Come All Ye Faithful" is "The
International Carol." This description is well deserved because of
its status as a top-ranking worldwide favorite and also because of its
indebtedness (real and erroneous) to several diverse cultures. The
original language was Latin, it was composed in France by an
Englishman, the Portuguese helped to spread it, and Germany and
Italy have been incorrectly connected to it. No other carol can
match the international mix of "O Come All Ye Faithful" and very
few can equal the influence of this "joyful and triumphant" tribute
to the Christmas season.

# O Come, O Come, Emmanuel

In Charles Dickens' famous novel *A Tale of Two Cities* there is a well-known line "It was the best of times, it was the worst of times . . . ." The enigma posed by this seemingly contradictory statement can also be found in another famous work of Western culture, the Advent carol "O Come, O Come, Emmanuel." For the history of the song could well be characterized by the statement "It was the oldest of carols, it was the newest of carols." It is old because both words and music are presumed to be from about the twelfth century, which would make it the oldest of the great carols, but there is no proof of this. (The country of its origin is unknown, although there are some hints that the music, at least, may be from France.) It is new because the lyrics and melody were not assembled into a carol until the middle of the nineteenth century.

John Mason Neale (1818-1866), an English clergyman, Greek and Latin scholar, and hymn writer, did a considerable amount of work on Christmas music. He was intimately associated with the creation of a number of carols, including "Good Christian Men, Rejoice" (1853) and "Good King Wenceslas" (1853). In 1851 he translated some Latin verses entitled "Veni, Emmanuel" and produced the well-known lyrics "O Come, O Come, Emmanuel." Three years later, in 1854, his associate Thomas Helmore (1811-1890) arranged some music of uncertain origin to go with Neale's lyrics, and the superlative international song was published. The tune, which is said to be adapted from plainsong, possibly could have been derived from a fifteenth-century processional used by Franciscan nuns, and if so, the music is about three centuries newer than is commonly believed. If this was the melody used by Helmore, and if it is from France as suspected, the music would be early modern. Furthermore, the Latin words, which are conjectured to be derived from short sixth- or seventh-century verses called "O Antiphons," can only be traced back as far as 1710, and so there is no real evidence that they are from the medieval era either. In reality, then, what Neale and Helmore created was a medieval carol of nineteenth-century origin. Due to strong identity with two different eras, an appropriate description for this anachronism might be "a carol of two centuries."

The uncertainty and contradictions in its historical background, though, have not detracted from its effectiveness and popularity as a Christmastime song. Neale's antiquated lyrics fit well with the old style of the music, although some of his verses are usually replaced by verses from a translation by Henry Sloane Coffin (1877-1954). And the smooth-flowing, mystical, hauntingly beautiful melody is magnificent. In mood and style, there is no other holiday song like it except possibly the early hymn, "Of the Father's Love Begotten." Because of its unique spiritual qualities, it could be called the musical soul of the Christmas season.

# Of the Father's Love Begotten

Probably the oldest significant carol lyric is "Veni, Redemptor gentium" ("Savior of the Nations, Come"), most likely written by the illustrious early Christian personage Saint Ambrose (340?-397). Soon after that, probably in the first part of the fifth century, two other notable Latin carol poems were written by Aurelius Clemens Prudentius (348-ca. 413). These were "O sola magnarum urbium" ("Earth Has Many a Noble City") and "Corde natus ex Parentis" ("Of the Father's Love Begotten" or "From the Father's Love Begotten").

Prudentius, a well-educated Spaniard, was a lawyer, a judge, and eventually chief of Emperor Honorius' imperial bodyguard. Toward the end of his life, he decided to exchange the temporal for the spiritual and withdraw to a monastery. In his new environment he immersed in contemplative and literary pursuits, including presumably his two enduring carols. "Corde natus" is the better known of the pair, and despite its great age is still fairly commonly used in the twentieth century, usually set to an anonymous and esthetic thirteenth-century plainsong. Its most familiar English translation, "Of the Father's Love Begotten," is by John Mason Neale (1818-1866), revised by Henry Williams Baker (1821-1877).

"Corde natus" is living and vital documentation that a carol can be stretched all the way from antiquity to the modern age and still flourish. Although it does not reach as high in artistry as its lofty spiritual cousin, "O Come, O Come, Emmanuel," this fine worship hymn offers us a special blend of history and faith that should be spared from the crushing motion of the fleeing centuries. May it still be remembered in another millennium and a half.

# Thou Didst Leave Thy Throne

Normally we do not think of Jesus' birth on this planet in relation to what the Son of God left behind. In an 1864 poem, however, English hymnist Emily Elizabeth Steele Elliott (1836-1897) artistically emphasized the sacrifices of Jesus in the sensitive and spiritual lines, "Thou didst leave Thy throne, and Thy kingly crown, When Thou camest to earth for me." This somewhat unconventional worship carol is the primary literary legacy by Elliott, who was the daughter of a rector in Brighton, England, and the niece of Charlotte Elliott (1789-1871), the author of the abundantly-used 1835 hymn "Just as I Am, Without One Plea."

The melody usually affixed to "Thou Didst Leave Thy Throne" is an 1876 composition by Timothy Richard Matthews (1826-1910), a clergyman in the Church of England and an amateur organist. The combination of Elliott's superior lyrics and Matthews' creditable tune has resulted in a very good but somewhat underpublicized carol. Hopefully, future Christmas celebrants will find more room in their hearts for this song, in the same spirit as Elliott's oft-repeated last line, "There is room in my heart for Thee."

# Wake, Awake, for Night Is Flying

Philipp Nicolai (1556-1608) was one of the more active German pastors of his era. He was also one of the more important contributors to the carol genre from any era. His two famous 1599 hymncarols, "How Brightly Beams the Morning Star" ("Wie schön leuchtet der Morgenstern") and "Wake, Awake, for Night Is Flying" ("Wachet auf! Ruft uns die Stimme") have several points in common in addition to the obvious ones of authorship and date.

Both are among the better hymns produced in Germany. Both have a high degree of positive spirituality. Both contain allusions to the night, perhaps engendered by the atmosphere of death prevalent in Unna, Germany, where Nicolai lived at the time. (This morbid condition was the direct aftermath of a serious 1597-1598 epidemic of bubonic plague.) Both have received extremely complimentary regal titles, with "How Brightly Beams" being called the "Queen of the chorales" and "Wake, Awake" being called the "King of the chorales." Both have their dominant English translations from the pen of Catherine Winkworth (1827-1878), the foremost carol translator from Great Britain, and both have been artistically utilized by Johann Sebastian Bach (1685-1750), the seemingly ubiquitous adapter of German music. In the case of "Wake, Awake," the words and music were inserted in the Cantata No. 140 (1731).

Despite its designation as the "king" and its wide appreciation as a worship carol, "Wake, Awake" is probably less popular as a Christmas song than the "Queen." And both are surely not as well received as another German Christmas chorale of the same century, Martin Luther's "From Heaven Above to Earth I Come," which has no title of royalty. Furthermore, all three are clearly less popular than some sixteenth-century carols of humble folk origins, for example, "The First Nowell," "God Rest You Merry, Gentlemen," and "We Wish You a Merry Christmas."

# SPIRITUALS

## Children, Go Where I Send Thee!

Black Americans have produced a hefty share of the music of the United States. Jazz is highly popular in America and throughout much of the world, and the black spiritual, which possibly developed in the eighteenth century, is a meaningful part of the American religious music tradition. Apparently an amalgamation of white spirituals and African music, black spirituals, including carols, are typically emotional, frequently inventive, generally tuneful, and sometimes poignant.

One of the better-known black spiritual carols is "Children, Go Where I Send Thee!," also known as "The Holy Baby" and "Little Bitty Baby." Probably created in the nineteenth century, it has two suspected places of origin. Because its two tunes are believed to be from Kentucky and Arkansas, one of those two states is presumed to be the source of the carol.

The most distinctive element of "Children" is its delightful counting feature. With its progressive device, "One for the little bitty Baby," "Two for Paul and Silas," "Three for the Hebrew Children," and so forth until reaching "Ten for the Ten Commandments," it is somewhat reminiscent of another carol. Its mate in musical mathematics is "The Twelve Days of Christmas," which also employs the technique of verse accumulation. The English folk carol, however, deals with the materialistic acquisition of holiday gifts while the American piece deals with religious concepts.

# Go Tell It on the Mountain

Enthusiasm pervades this truly splendid black spiritual. Probably created in the late nineteenth century or early twentieth century, the vigorous, full-bodied, and highly moving nature of this folk master-piece has made it one of the up-and-coming favorites of the holiday season. In roughly a century it has carved a substantial niche for itself without benefit of the pop music or conventional religious establish-ments. What is the secret of "Go Tell It on the Mountain"? Simply, it is an aggregate of very positive "e" words. Add to enthusiastic the terms energetic, ebullient, exciting, emphatic, esthetic, and excellent as well as others, and you have a true composite of the song.

Although generally considered as anonymous, this fine musical work may have been composed by a person named Work. Nashville-born Frederick Jerome Work (1880-1942), a black composer, teach-er, and scholar has been attributed as the author of the song by his equally accomplished nephew, John Wesley Work (1901-1967). This claim is hard to prove either way. Both men were intimately and substantially affiliated with the collection, arrangement, and disse-mination of black spirituals, and John Work adapted the lyrics and the music of "Go Tell." Most likely, Frederick Work only discovered and preserved the song, but it is possible that he was the author of this inspired jewel, the greatest of all American folk carols.

# I Wonder as I Wander

The distinction between folk and mainstream music can be quite hazy. This is certainly the situation for the extremely beautiful white spiritual carol, "I Wonder as I Wander." In part it is from the folk domain, since the first lines of the words and the inspiration for the remainder of the lyrics and for the tune came from a folk song heard in North Carolina. In largest part, though, it is from the talents of John Jacob Niles (1892-1980), who took the folk threads he witnessed and wove them into a tapestry of exceptional artistry.

Niles, a famous Kentucky-born folk singer, collector of folk music, and composer, also wrote some other carols by using the same basic technique. "Jesus, Jesus, Rest Your Head," created in 1932, is perhaps the best known of the others. But of all his extensive activities relating to folk music, his 1933 carol, "I Wonder," has brought him the most recognition. Such attention is very well justified, for the song is unique in character and absolutely haunting and esthetically chilling when sung by a suitable high soprano. Decidedly spiritual in tone and ethereal in sensation, "I Wonder" is one of the very top carols of the twentieth century. That a piece drenched with pathos could penetrate the generally happy superstructure of holiday music is something of a miracle. Yet after all, isn't Christmas a time for miracles?

# The Last Month of the Year

Two factors can immensely help the long-term success of a carol. No matter what other assets or liabilities a carol may have, an exceptionally attractive tune or an imaginative literary device will normally carry the song a considerable distance toward the pinnacle of posterity. The primary means of transport for "The Last Month of the Year" are the novelty of listing all of the 12 months and a title which is both catchy and original. No other known carol uses a title even roughly equivalent.

The author of this song in black spiritual style was probably Vera Hall (1905-1964), who was born in, and died in, Livingston, Alabama. In the early part of her life she was simply a domestic servant, but later on her songs gained the attention of the outstanding American folklorist John Avery Lomax (1867-1948), who recorded some of her music for the Library of Congress' American Archive of Folk Song. "Last Month" 's first-known publication was 1953, but it is suspected that the carol was created much earlier, quite possibly in the 1920s or 1930s. One indicator of the song's appreciable usage is the appearance of two variant titles, "January, February," and "What Month Was My Jesus Born In?" within a time span of roughly two generations.

# Mary Had a Baby

No different from other types of Christmas songs, carols from Black-American sources frequently employ the theme of Mary. Among such works are "Oh, Mary, Where Is Your Baby?," "Mary, What Are You Going to Name That Pretty Little Baby?," and "Mary Had a Baby," all folk pieces, plus "Mary's Little Boy Child" by Jester Hairston (1901- ). There is a difference of emphasis between the two groups, though, with the carols from black sources appearing to have an especial fascination and affection for the fragile image of the blessed young woman and her helpless holy infant.

"Mary Had a Baby," probably conceived in the nineteenth century, may have originated in South Carolina, a particularly rich repository for the creation of black spiritual carols. Definitely one of the better pieces of its type, "Mary Had a Baby" is noted for an ending that contains a precious bit of folk profundity. Notwithstanding its informal and humble background, the spiritual sports one of the more interesting and perceptive lines in any Christmas song. Ingenuously and almost casually tossed out at the conclusion of each stanza is the theologically provocative observation, "O Lord, the people keep a-comin' and the train done gone."

# Rise Up, Shepherd, and Follow

At first glance, it might appear that the lovely song "Rise Up, Shepherd, and Follow" is a typical carol. Like most American folk carols, it probably dates from the vague chronological expanse of the eighteenth or nineteenth centuries. In its content, there is nothing particularly out of the ordinary, with normal biblical allusions such as shepherds and the star being the focus of the lyrics.

On further examination, though, the song gives the impression of being atypical in some ways. It was published in 1867, only two years after the Civil War, while most black spiritual carols were not put into print until the twentieth century. It is also commonly performed in an uncommon manner. The verses are frequently sung by a soloist, with an ensemble of voices singing the key phrase, "Rise up, shepherd, and follow" in response. It furthermore is marred by two errors of fact in the otherwise good words. The shepherds are described as seeing the star of Bethlehem, when that nocturnal phenomenon really was viewed by the Wise Men, and it chooses the terminology "star in the East," when the star was probably in the West and followed by men coming from the East. The mistake comes from the misinterpretation of the portion of Matthew 2:2 which says "we have seen his star in the East." If the star was actually in the eastern sky, the Wise Men would have most likely traversed the Mediterranean Sea, while if the star was in the western sky, they could have begun the journey from any of the many lands of west Asia. This logic is entirely consistent with Matthew 2:1 which indicates that the Wise Men came from the East.

These misconceptions are far from unique to "Rise Up, Shepherd, and Follow." The great song "The First Nowell" also contains both of the mistakes, and other carols are by no means free of this type of misimpression. So it might be preferable to categorize the textual faults of "Rise Up, Shepherd" as quite typical of the carol genre, instead of something new.

# CHRISTMAS JOY

## All My Heart This Night Rejoices

In the affections of German Lutherans no figure in hymnody outranks the great reformer Martin Luther (1483-1546). But there is another German hymn writer who does somewhat compare with Luther in acceptance by this group. Paul Gerhardt (1607-1676), a Lutheran minister and author of 132 hymns, is one of the most popular and influential hymnists from Germany. His best-known song, "Fröhlich soll mein Herze springen," published in 1653 while he was pastor at Mittenwalde, is an enduring contribution to the songs of Christmas.

Several melodies have been linked with Gerhardt's lyrics. One of their more common mates is a 1666 tune by Johann Georg Ebeling (1637-1676), a German composer and music teacher. A contemporary of Gerhardt, Ebeling provided settings for 120 of Gerhardt's hymns. Another well-known companion to Gerhardt's poem is a composition by American Horatio Parker (1863-1919), an organist, choirmaster, and accomplished composer who created his melody in 1894 at about the time he became chair of music at Yale University.

The most popular English-language version of Gerhardt's hymn, "All My Heart This Night Rejoices," is by Catherine Winkworth (1827-1878), a hymn translator from England whose skill at her craft has brought her lasting fame. In either German or English, the words devoutly express the religious joys of Christmas observance. What makes this carol even more exceptional is that it was generated by a soul which was deeply marked by much personal tragedy and by the disturbing conflicts of the time, including the bloody

Thirty Years' War (1618-1648), which ceased just a few years before. Optimism arising like the phoenix from the ashes of negativism is always welcome, especially in the positive environment of the holiday season.

# Christians, Awake, Salute the Happy Morn

It is unlikely that Englishman John Byrom (1692-1763) wrote his well-known 1749 Christmas poem in shorthand. But he could have, for seven years earlier he copyrighted an important early system of notation called the Universal English Shorthand. Multifaceted Byrom also was a trained physician (nonpracticing) and a very skillful writer who contributed to the famous periodical, *The Spectator.*

In December of 1749, Byrom, who was a friend of Charles Wesley (another poet of consequence), as well as Charles' brother John, wrote "Christians, Awake, Salute the Happy Morn." Reportedly, it was conceived in response to a Christmas gift request by his daughter, Dolly. One year later, in December 1750, another friend, organist and composer John Wainwright (1723-1768), composed a setting for Byrom's poem. Accompanied by a group of "singing men and boys," Wainwright came to Byrom's home on Christmas morning and serenaded the family with the new carol. The idiosyncrasies of this moderately popular carol do not end with these two cheerful Christmas Day surprises or with the unusual background of its lyricist. The words, which are narrative in style and joyous in mood, are also rather eccentric in literary content. Furthermore, the good march-like music by Wainwright has over the years acquired an odd appendage. Its dominant tune name, "Yorkshire," is quite misleading since Wainwright lived in Cheshire and had absolutely no connection with the other county. If such a discrepancy is disturbing to anybody, one of the variant tune names could be selected. There are, after all, only ten other names to choose from.

# Good Christian Men, Rejoice

Reverend John Mason Neale (1818-1866) was a bit odd. It can easily be granted that he is one of the greatest propagators of the Christmas carol because of his personal development of three top carols, and that his accomplishments in the entire field of hymnody are prodigious. Yet there is something patently quaint about the London-born Anglican priest who never attained a parish position due to a combination of chronically poor health and Anglo-Catholic theological tendencies, who was the warden of a home for old men in Sussex, and whose principal preoccupations were the realms of Greek and Latin. His three famous carols are clear illustrations of his idiosyncratic qualities. "O Come, O Come, Emmanuel" is in effect a medieval carol that did not exist before the nineteenth century. "Good King Wenceslas" is a most peculiar blend of a delightful melody and horrible lyrics. And "Good Christian Men, Rejoice" is essentially pirated from another leading carol.

The song from which Neale extracted "Good Christian Men, Rejoice" is, like Neale, decidedly esoteric. In 1853 Neale published a free paraphrase of the macaronic (combined Latin and vernacular) fourteenth-century jewel "In dulci jubilo," which is by tradition reputed to have been the offspring of angelic singing and dancing. By using the same spirited melody that was affixed to the earlier carol, Neale was assured that his "new" song of joy would be successful. Although some doubts could be cast on various aspects of Neale's life and activities, his attachment of lyrics to the exceptional melodies for "O Come, O Come, Emmanuel," "Good King Wenceslas," and "Good Christian Men, Rejoice" leave no question as to his ability to recognize good tunes.

# The Happy Christmas Comes Once More

The fairy tales of Hans Christian Andersen (1805-1875) are often the image evoked when the arts and intellectual life of Denmark are touched upon. Andersen's literary work, though, is only a very small part of a large body of fine artistic and intellectual endeavor from that small Scandinavian nation. Other activities that are internationally appreciated include: the philosophy of the very influential Soren Kierkegaard (1813-1855); the production of ballets; and the creation of serious music including the work of Carl Nielsen (1865-1931) and some notable nineteenth-century ballet music. And the Danes have produced their share of good Christmas carols, although no Danish carol is a renowned worldwide favorite.

There are several Christmas songs of note from Denmark. "Barn Jesus," ("Child Jesus"), a mid-nineteenth-century carol, has lyrics by none other than Hans Christian Andersen and music by one of Denmark's most famous composers, Niels Wilhelm Gade (1817-1890); "Deilig er den himmel blaa" ("Lovely is the Dark Blue Sky") pairs words by Nicolai Frederik Severin Grundtwig (1783-1872) with a modern Danish folk tune; and "Det kimer nu til Julefest" ("The Happy Christmas Comes Once More") combines another set of lyrics by Grundtwig with music by Carl C. N. Balle (1806-1855). This last song is perhaps Denmark's best-known carol.

Grundtwig, who was a prominent educator, minister, and champion of mass education as well as a highly productive writer, published the lyrics for this joyous carol in 1817. While Grundtwig is one of Denmark's most famous personages, Balle, who published his melody in 1850, is obscure. Grundtwig's contribution to this carol was a minuscule part of his life. In contrast, Balle's contribution was his one shot into history.

# I Am So Glad on Christmas Eve

Norway is famous for its magnificent fjords, and the plays of Henrik Ibsen (1828-1906), and the music of Edvard Grieg (1843-1907). Norway is not famous for its Christmas songs. Only one carol from Norway has particularly gained the attention of the international music community. This rarity is the nineteenth-century song, "Jeg er saa glad hver Julekveld" which is variously translated as "I Am So Glad on Christmas Eve," "I Am So Glad Each Christmas Eve," "How Glad I Am Each Christmas Eve," "When Lights Are Lit on Christmas Eve," and "Christmas Eve."

"I Am So Glad" is a very good carol, with flowing music by the obscure composer Peder Knudsen (1819-1863) and with joyful lyrics by the equally obscure Marie Wexelsen (1832-1911). In theme it is roughly similar, perhaps not by coincidence, to the most famous carols of Norway's sister Scandinavian nations, Denmark and Sweden. The same concept of delight with the approach of the holiday is also found in Denmark's leading carol, "Det kimer nu til Julefest" ("The Happy Christmas Comes Once More") and Sweden's leading carol, "Nu är det Jul igen" ("Christmas Is Here Again" or "Dance Carol"). From this pattern it is apparent that the Scandinavians not only share related languages and somewhat comparable climates, but also have a common zest for the celebration of Christmas.

# In Dulci Jubilo

Angels have frequently been a topic in Christmas carols. Angels have very seldom been reported as the inspiration for carols. Lewis Redner suggested that his excellent tune for "O Little Town of Bethlehem" may have been sent by the winged attendants of Heaven. Also, there is a legend that the German Dominican mystic Heinrich Suso (d. 1366) not only contacted the angels but danced with them and sang a song with them. After this interlude, the story continues, Suso wrote down the tune and lyrics of the angelic song, and the famous carol "In dulci jubilo" was preserved for us mortals. Further assistance in preservation was rendered by a manuscript dating around 1400 and by a printed version dated 1533.

The sophisticates of the twentieth century may scoff at this dreamlike incident, but no matter what the exact circumstances of the composition of the fourteenth-century carol may have been, there is something in the legend that rings true. It hints that one way or another Suso may possibly have been the author of this exceptional Latin and German carol, which generally has been regarded as anonymous. In any case, this strong song is still very much a part of the holiday scene six centuries later. The Latin words are still retained, with the German lyrics converted in English-speaking countries to a widely used translation by Robert Lucas de Pearsall (1795-1856). Another even better-known English-language treatment of the carol is the paraphrase made by John Mason Neale (1818-1866). With Neale's poetic adaptation attached to the fourteenth-century tune, another famous carol, "Good Christian Men, Rejoice," became hybridized.

In whatever form the carol may be performed, it is a joyous and pleasurable addition to the month of December. As the translation of the Latin testifies, the song is tastefully wrapped "in sweet jubilation."

# Joy to the World!

"Genius" and "at his best . . . unapproachable" are accolades not dispensed to everyone who has taken pen in hand. These lofty plaudits plus "the bard of Southampton" and "father of English hymnody" have been showered upon Isaac Watts (1674-1748), the author of "Joy to the World!" Only one other English-language hymnwriter, Charles Welsey, the lyricist for "Hark! The Herald Angels Sing," is seriously compared to Watts. If a choice had to be made as to which of these two great hymnists has made the larger historical contribution, the decision would probably go to Watts.

A nonconformist pastor and prodigious author of theological and philosophical books (about 60) and hymns (about 700), Watts is most remembered for the extraordinary hymns, "When I Survey the Wondrous Cross," "Our God Our Help in Ages Past," and "Joy to the World!" The renowned nineteenth-century English author Matthew Arnold considered "When I Survey" to be the best hymn in the English language. "Our God" has been described as "England's second national anthem," and "Joy" ranks in the very top level of Christmas songs. First published in Watts' 1719 work, *The Psalms of David, Imitated in the Language of the New Testament*, "Joy" was a paraphrase of the second part of Psalm 98. Originally the opening line read "Joy to the earth," but eventually the better term "world" entirely supplanted "earth."

Over a century after Watts' carol lyrics first appeared, it was printed with a splendid, dynamic tune in an 1839 collection entitled *The Modern Psalmist*. The sole indication of authorship for the melody was the cryptic notation "from Handel." Because of this strange wording and some similarities between parts of the tune and parts of the *Messiah*, the superlative 1742 choral work by George Frederick Handel (1685-1759), the melody has almost universally been attributed to the English music master. Yet the links to Handel are very weak and tenuous and scholars have basically refuted the hypothesis of Handelian authorship.

The probable composer of the tune for "Joy" was Lowell Mason (1792-1872), a prominent American music educator, music editor, and hymn writer. In Mason's background there are three elements that tend to support the suspicion that he was responsible for the melody. First, he was deeply immersed in the music of such classical composers as Handel, Haydn, Mozart, and Beethoven, and readily commuted between their domain and his own creativity. Second, Mason had a decided tendency toward anonymity, and many of his own compositions were unsigned. Supposedly, he was the "arranger" of the 1824 tune which is commonly used with another of Watts' hymns, "When I Survey the Wondrous Cross," but various factors very strongly tempt one to believe that Mason actually composed the 1824 melody. Third, Mason was a hymn tune composer of some accomplishment. On top of the strong possibility that he produced the tune for "When I Survey," he is definitely credited with the composition of the good tunes for "My Faith Looks Up to Thee" and "Nearer, My God, to Thee." Add to these three characteristics the fact that Mason was the editor of the 1839 collection in which the tune for "Joy" first appeared, and a fairly convincing case for Mason can be assembled. Apparently, Mason was influenced by Handel during the creation of the melody, and quite possibly was sincerely unsure where the dividing line between Handel and himself really was. Hence the misleading notation in the 1839 collection evolved, followed perhaps predictably by the folklore concerning Handel. (To compound the confusion, recent research has indicated that Mason was not only under the influence of Handel, but may also have "borrowed" the tune from yet another source.)

In spite of the uncertainty about the tune's origins, there is no doubt that the carol synthesized by the joint talents of the father of English hymnody and the father of American hymnologic anonymity has few peers in quality or international popularity. Both words and music, carried along by extremely esthetic conveyances of term and tone, joyfully proclaim the birth of Jesus. Of all the sacred carols, "Joy" is perhaps the most positive and uplifting declaration of the message of Christmas. The exclamation point almost universally inserted by carol editors after the initial line, "Joy to the world!," powerfully punctuates the exhilarating effect that this carol has had for the past century and a half.

# Masters in This Hall

It is said that the English Renaissance ended in the mid-seventeenth century. Yet some of the marvelous spirit of that superlative era did not die, for two centuries later, in the heart of the Victorian era, a veritable Renaissance man flourished. With fine accomplishments in poetry, in several areas of the visual arts, and in printing, as well as active participation in social reform and politics, William Morris (1834-1896) was one of the most versatile talents of his or any age. One of his minor achievements was the composition of the lyrics for "Masters in This Hall," which for a much lesser person would have preserved a small bit of immortality, but which for Morris was probably just a temporarily diverting artistic aside.

It took two middlemen to start the process of Morris' carol composition. The first was the organist at Chartres Cathedral in northwest France. The organist gave an energetic folk tune, possibly from the Chartres area, to the English carol compiler Edmund Sedding (1835-1868). The second middleman Sedding then carried the tune to his associate Morris, and asked the multifaceted artist to make a poetic setting for the tune. The resultant carol was published by Sedding in an 1860 collection.

Today, the song is a relatively popular international carol, though by no means in the first rank of public acceptance. The mainstay of the song is its vibrant and lively tune which, by best guess, comes from the seventeenth or eighteenth century. Morris' lyrics, on the other hand, are somewhat of a curiosity. Although well-crafted and appropriate to the music, they do remind the listener more of the sixteenth century than the nineteenth. It appears that Morris was not only a Renaissance man in the breadth of his endeavors, but also at least to some extent in the depth of his highly creative powers.

# O Thou Joyful Day

What well-known Christmas carol is a direct descendant of a major non-Christmas song, has four siblings with close ties, and has a melody whose title unjustifiably implies relationships with Italy and the sea? The answer to this trivia puzzler about musical relatives is the anonymous song, "O Thou Joyful Day." Probably written in the United States in the nineteenth century, this carol has three similar English-language kin all under the title, "O Sanctissima," and one German-language relation under the title, "O du fröhliche." The affiliated English-language carols are all twentieth century and American, two anonymous and one by William Glass. The German carol, by Johannes Daniel Falk (1768-1826), was published in 1816. Its several English translations, for example, "O How Joyfully," collectively emphasize the joyfulness of the German original.

All of these five songs are derived from an anonymous sixteenth-century Latin hymn of praise to the Virgin Mary, "O Sanctissima." The source of inspiration for the five Christmas carols was, therefore, a piece without any direct connection to the holiday. Equally ironic is the tune, "Sicilian Mariners," which is the music for all six lyrics under discussion. In spite of the suggestion of association with Sicily and maritime matters, no linkage with either has been proven. The melody was probably created in the second half of the eighteenth century, possibly from folk sources, possibly from an obscure opera.

The tune first appeared, as far as is known, in *Improved Psalmody* (1794), edited by Englishman William Tattersall (1752-1829). Since then it has been widely appreciated and widely adapted. The immortal Ludwig van Beethoven (1770-1827) devoted some of his genius to making an arrangement of it, and it has been utilized for a standard hymn, "Lord, Dismiss Us with Thy Blessing" (1773), as well as for other hymns. Overall, it is one of the more popular and artistically superior tunes of any era, and its buoyant, dynamic, and sweeping nature is a perfect match for the several carols it has graced. In the United States, "O Thou Joyful Day" is the most familiar of "Sicilian Mariner"'s stable of Christmas songs, but, worldwide, Falk's "O du fröhliche" may possibly be better known.

# PART II:
# CHRISTMAS AS A HOLIDAY

# WINTER FUN

## Let It Snow! Let It Snow! Let It Snow!

Although it is almost certain that the birth of Jesus did not occur during the winter, the adoption of the period of the December solstice as the Christmas holiday has decidedly enhanced the scope and enjoyment of this very important point on the calendar. The invigorating experiences of snow and ice, and the comfort of retreat to the warmth of the fireplace, continue to strongly stimulate the sentiments and imaginations of holiday participants. So songs about snow and the winter season, although not specifically referring to Christmas, can be very relevant to the December celebrations.

One of the most delightful of this type of song is "Let It Snow! Let It Snow! Let It Snow!," a 1945 composition by New York City-born lyricist Sammy Cahn (1913-1992) and London-born composer Jule Styne (1905-1994). Both men were very successful in the American popular music arena, with Cahn also writing the words for the award-winning songs "Love and Marriage" (1955), "All the Way" (1957), "Call Me Irresponsible" (1963), and "High Hopes" (1959), and Styne composing the music for the Broadway shows *Gentlemen Prefer Blondes* (1949), *Bells Are Ringing* (1956), *Gypsy* (1959), and *Funny Girl* (1964), as well as for a variety of songs. Another well-known piece on which Cahn and Styne collaborated was the Academy Award-winning song, "Three Coins in the Fountain," which they wrote in 1954, the same year they produced their moderately well-known song with "Christmas" actually in the title, "The Christmas Waltz." With all these noted endeavors, it could be easy to overlook the bouncy and affable little wintertime morsel they created. Fortunately, its annual renewal as a tiny stream in the mighty flow of holiday music allows us to enjoy its white warmth over and over.

# A Marshmallow World

One of the more original and picturesque images of the winter scene can be found in Carl Sigman's 1949 lyric, "A Marshmallow World." Brooklyn-born Sigman (1909- ) concocted this sugary and soft depiction of a snowfall in concert with New York City-born composer Peter De Rose (1900-1953). This was Sigman's and De Rose's only known collaboration. Independently, however, Sigman wrote words and/or music for a diverse array of popular pieces including "Ballerina" or "Dance Ballerina Dance" (1947), "Enjoy Yourself, It's Later Than You Think" (1948), "Bongo, Bongo, Bongo" (1947), "Ebb Tide" (1953), "Pennsylvania 6-5000" (1939), "My Heart Cries for You" (1950), and "Arrivederci, Roma" (1958). On his own, De Rose is best known for the excellent 1934 piano piece, "Deep Purple" to which lyrics were later attached.

Certainly "A Marshmallow World" cannot be listed among the finer or more prestigious songs of Christmas. With considerable justification, it could be characterized as a pleasant piece of holiday fluff (pun intended). Yet it is one of the better treatments of winter ever to have emanated from the world of popular music. As long as we continue to have the type of weather sketched in this lively holiday favorite, it is hoped that this type of song continues to brighten our end-of-the-year environment.

# Sleigh Ride

Mitchell Parish (1900-1993) appears to have possessed a rare talent. The lyricist from Shreveport, Louisiana, had a certain knack for associating with songs of especially high caliber and fame. He provided the words for no less than four American popular classics–"Stardust" (music 1927, words 1929) with Hoagy Carmichael, "Deep Purple" (music 1934, words 1939) with Peter De Rose, "Moonlight Serenade" (1939) with Glenn Miller, and "Sleigh Ride" with Leroy Anderson. Some other familiar songs, including the 1965 Christmas piece, "The White World of Winter," written with composer Hoagy Carmichael, were also products of his collaborative talents.

His creative mate on "Sleigh Ride" was not exactly a one-song phenomenon either. Anderson (1908-1975), born in Cambridge, Massachusetts, was one of the most gifted semi-classical composers ever to grace the United States. "Fiddle Faddle"(1948), "The Syncopated Clock" (1950), "Bugler's Holiday" (1954), "The Typewriter" (1953), "Serenata" (1949), "Blue Tango" (1952), and other imaginative works brought him much fame and respect. He was appreciated as a popular and a classical composer, with groups like the Boston Pops Orchestra dedicating programs to him. "Sleigh Ride," composed in 1948, was one of his best efforts. Initially it was solely an instrumental work, and it still is frequently performed that way, but in 1950 Parish performed his habitual act of lyricizing with winners. As a song with words, "Sleigh Ride" is in the top rank of popular Christmas carols with mood and theme similar to "Jingle Bells," but with definite artistic superiority over the earlier song. As an orchestral work, it is a very fine contribution to the music of the season. In style and imagery it is a lot like another and even better instrumental composition, "Troika," from Sergei Prokofiev's 1934 masterpiece, Lieutenant Kije, which exhilaratingly depicts a ride in a three-horse open sleigh.

# Winter Wonderland

There is nothing gimmicky or exotic about the theme of "Winter Wonderland." To the contrary, the picture of a couple in love strolling though the romantic setting of a snowy winter day is rather commonplace. It is an experience which so many of us, including surely the authors of the song, have enjoyed at one time or another. Perhaps the pleasant familiarity of hearing sleigh bells, seeing glistening snow, building a snowman, and dreaming by a fire is a good part of the success of this perennial holiday charmer. Yet at least equally responsible for its strong continuance year after year are its very skillful lyrics and melody.

"Winter Wonderland" was by far the best effort of lyricist Richard B. Smith (1901-1935) and of composer Felix Bernard (1897-1944). Ironically, neither man had much opportunity to savor the sweet rewards from their highly popular 1934 song. Pennsylvania-born Smith died the very next year, and Brooklyn-born Bernard did not live a lot longer, passing away about ten years later. Neither was around for the cheerful best-selling 1950 recording by the Andrews Sisters. So in the midst of the warmth, happiness, and personalness of this lyrical little carol is a definite flaw of tragedy, particularly pertaining to Smith.

# HOLIDAY GREETINGS

## God Rest You Merry, Gentlemen

Charles Dickens (1812-1870) was England's greatest writer of fiction. The classic 1843 story *A Christmas Carol* was Dickens' best-loved work as well as the most famous piece of Christmas literature except for the biblical account of the Nativity. Dickens' tale is so familiar in English-speaking countries that few persons are not acquainted with the characters of Scrooge, Bob Cratchit, and Tiny Tim. But at the same time most persons are probably not aware that a famous carol plays a significant role in Dickens' masterful narrative. Toward the beginning of the story, while Scrooge was in his counting house, a young London street inhabitant serenaded the old miser with the lines, "God bless you merry gentlemen! May nothing you dismay!" Scrooge responded by ferociously chasing the lad away.

"God Rest You Merry, Gentlemen" is, therefore, the Christmas carol of *A Christmas Carol*. And it is quite appropriate that Dickens chose that particular song, for no other carol has had a stronger cultural effect on London and on England as a whole than the spiritual piece which infringed on Scrooge's grouchy privacy. The very streets of London which were the locale for Dickens' diorama were probably the source of this great folk carol. Quite possibly the persons responsible for its creation were the Waits of London, a city-supported band of long tradition, and it is strongly suspected that both words and music came out of the highly fertile sixteenth century.

Apparently the song was not published until the eighteenth century, at which time some major variations in the lyrics developed.

Originally lines three and four read, "For Jesus Christ our Saviour was born upon this day," but starting in the eighteenth century the lines "Remember Christ our Saviour was born on Christmas Day" began to be substituted for the same lines. Both variants are commonly used today. Another eighteenth-century change was the composition of a variant tune, a folk melody from Cornwall in the west of England. The Cornwall tune is used only sparingly, as is another variant tune by Lewis Henry Redner (1831-1908), the composer of the original melody for "O Little Town of Bethlehem." It is not at all surprising that other tunes tried with "God Rest" have not caught on, for the simple sixteenth-century melody is dynamically exquisite and humbly magnificent, and has an alluring touch of mystery and exoticism. The lyrics exude similar sensations and are generally quite pleasant in spite of such archaic passages as "In Bethlehem in Jewry" and "The which his mother Mary did nothing take in scorn."

There have been, however, two major misunderstandings relating to the words. The first one involves the placement of the comma in the initial line. The punctuation was intended to follow "merry" which would give the line the meaning "God keep you in good spirits, gentlemen." Frequently, though, the comma is misplaced after "you," thus allowing for the interpretation "God give you rest, merry-making gentlemen." The second misimpression involves the tone of the text. The carol is from the beginning to the end completely religious in content, but has often been treated as a secular invitation to participate in the hedonistic festivities of the holidays. In part this error is due to the bold cheerfulness of the salutation, in part to the misplacement of the comma, in part to the terminology of the refrain ("O tidings of comfort and joy"), and in part to the vivacious and uplifting melody which accompanies the lyrics.

There are few misunderstandings, however, about the long-term effect and popularity of this international favorite. It is quite possibly the leading carol of completely English origins, with only "The First Nowell" at all competing for this distinction, and stands prominently in the front row of Christmas music. With some persons, including this author, it is no less than number one in their affections. Some other carols may overall be more esthetic, but few, if any, offer a richer feast of spiritual and psychological comfort and joy.

# Happy Holiday

Originally, "Happy Holiday" was connected not just with Christmas. When Irving Berlin (1888-1989) wrote this song in 1941 for the 1942 musical film *Holiday Inn*, it was intended to serve as a generic piece to cover a dozen holidays. But its association with this movie, which has become a Christmas standard, and with "White Christmas," the extremely popular ballad from the same movie, has caused the song to be absorbed into the seemingly insatiable musical appetite of the winter holiday.

"Happy Holiday" certainly is not the best work of the genius of Irving Berlin, the Russian-born immigrant with hardly any musical training. Compared to such classics as "Alexander's Ragtime Band" (1911), "Easter Parade" (1933), "A Pretty Girl Is Like a Melody" (1919), "Say It with Music" (1921), "Blue Skies" (1927), "I've Got My Love to Keep Me Warm" (1937), "There's No Business Like Show Business" (1946), and "God Bless America" (1939), "Happy Holiday" is a minor ditty. Yet it has a degree of irresistibility due to the triad of Christmas, Berlin, and Bing Crosby, who first sang it, plus the simple and direct affability of its cheery salutation.

# Have Yourself a Merry Little Christmas

The 1939 movie *The Wizard of Oz* is perhaps the most beloved of all Hollywood productions. In that film Judy Garland was introduced to the world by her role as Dorothy and by her rendition of "Over the Rainbow." Five years later, Garland returned the favor by introducing to the world another memorable song, "Have Yourself a Merry Little Christmas," in the 1944 movie *Meet Me in St. Louis.*

The authors of this merry little Christmas song were Alabama-born composer, lyricist, and singer Hugh Martin (1914- ), who wrote the music, and Oklahoma-born singer, lyricist, and composer Ralph Blane Hunsecker (1914- ), also known as Ralph Blane, who wrote the lyrics. Martin and Blane were frequent collaborators, also combining on "Buckle Down Winsocki" (1941), "The Trolley Song" (1944), "The Boy Next Door" (1944), and "Pass that Peace Pipe" (1948). ("Trolley Song" and "Boy Next Door" were also in *Meet Me in St. Louis.*) Their most enduring song, possibly, is "Have Yourself a Merry Little Christmas." In part this is because it is a pleasant and accessible piece of musical dreaminess, and in part because it is strongly entrenched in the December holiday season, a most favorable situation for the preservation of any song, including lesser ones than this ballad.

# A Holly Jolly Christmas

The most significant and successful composer of American Christmas songs since World War II is undoubtedly John D. ("Johnny") Marks (1909-1985). The Mt. Vernon, New York-born composer is most famous for the 1949 classic, "Rudolph the Red-Nosed Reindeer," but Marks' contributions to the holiday extend far beyond his celebrated leader of Santa's sleigh. Other music by Marks includes "A Merry, Merry Christmas to You" (1958), "Rockin' Around the Christmas Tree" (1958), "A Holly Jolly Christmas" (1962), "Silver and Gold" (1964), "A Caroling We Go" (1966), "The Most Wonderful Day of the Year" (1964), "When Santa Claus Gets Your Letter" (1950), "Jingle, Jingle, Jingle" (1964), and variant tunes for "I Heard the Bells on Christmas Day" and "'Twas the Night Before Christmas."

Outside of "Rudolph," "Rockin'" and "A Holly Jolly" are probably the most performed pieces, although his variant for "I Heard the Bells" also gets a moderate amount of attention. "A Holly Jolly" received a lot of publicity in 1964 when it was sung by Burl Ives in the highly popular and apparently perennial television special *Rudolph the Red-Nosed Reindeer*. With its friendly exhortation to "Have a holly jolly Christmas," it is a bouncy and cheerful song with a degree of durability on its own. Its appearance on millions of television sets each December can only add to its longevity.

# We Wish You a Merry Christmas

The considerable cultural impact of the Christmas carol is graphically demonstrated by the simple yet very popular folk carol from the West Country of England, "We Wish You a Merry Christmas." Although this song, which is quite possibly from the sixteenth century, is lively, attractive, affable, and conducive to the attainment of a positive holiday temperament, it cannot be considered as a piece with outstanding artistic substance.

The songs which are musically superior to "We Wish" are legion. But if one lists the songs which are better known, more performed, and more reacted to, they would certainly number far less than whatever number legion may be. There is just one reason for this discrepancy. "We Wish" is one of the primary elements in the body of music which pervades the longest, most beloved, and most culturally dominant of our holidays. Collectively, no other group of songs appears to have as much influence on Western civilization as do Christmas carols, especially in light of the relatively small number of significant carols that exist. Carols are not limited by age, education, life-style, beliefs, nationality, or taste.

For about one month of each year they strongly envelop all sectors of predominantly Christian nations, and even non-Christian areas are not exempt from their presence. A little song like "We Wish You a Merry Christmas," therefore, can have an effect surpassing its intrinsic merits because of its continuing membership in the highly influential club of carols.

# HOLIDAY FESTIVITIES

# Auld Lang Syne

One of the most widely sung pieces in the English language is "Auld Lang Syne," the Scottish-dialect tidbit which is ubiquitous in New Year's Eve celebrations. It is so familiar to our culture, it is such a fixture of our holiday season, that to delete it from our festivities might seem equivalent to sacrilege. Yet little is known about the song except that it is from Scotland, a land not famous for its carols, and that the great Scottish poet Robert Burns (1759-1796) wrote some of the verses.

The most familiar stanza, the first one, is of folk origins, as are some of the other verses. The folk verses probably date from the seventeenth century, although the sixteenth or eighteenth centuries are also possibilities. In 1788 Burns wrote two additional verses to the poem, and the association of his name with the work has consequently led to a common miscomprehension that the entire poem was from his talented pen. The tune first appeared with the lyrics in 1799, but is surely considerably older than that, conceivably as early as the sixteenth century. Since it is apparently of folk origins, and was not put into print until the eighteenth century, any effort at precise dating can only be speculative.

The fuzziness of its history may have contributed to the romance of this attractive old curiosity. We all sing it. We all are slightly amused and bemused about it. And we all are affected by the sentimentality of the lyrics that look back with fondness to "auld lang syne" ("old long since") and by the smooth, highly accessible melody which transports us there.

# The Boar's Head Carol

Believe it or not, there actually are two English carols called "The Boar's Head." One is a religious song probably composed by Richard Smert who lived in Devonshire, England in the second half of the fifteenth century. Little else is known about Smert except that he probably was the creator of another carol, "Sir Christmas." (Yes, reader, there was a Sir Christmas!) Smert's "The Boar's Head" apparently was a reaction to the secular and much better-known carol of the same century.

The other boarish song is usually called "The Boar's Head Carol" to distinguish it from the lesser-known one. Also known as "Carol on Bringing in the Boar's Head," "The Bore's Heed," and "Caput apri defero," it was one of the first carols to be printed. In 1521 it appeared in Wynken de Worde's collection, *Christmasse Carolles*. It probably was created about a century earlier, anonymously, and probably in Oxford, England. The presumption of its fifteenth-century Oxford origins is founded on the custom of singing the song in Christmas celebrations at Queen's College, Oxford, for well over 500 years.

Few carols, if any, surpass "The Boar's Head Carol" in the ingenuity and humor of its legendary origins. The tale is that a student at Queen's College was strolling in adjacent woods on Christmas Day and was accosted by a wild boar. The student killed the boar by thrusting a volume by Aristotle down the beast's throat. That evening the animal was served to the student body with considerable ceremony, thus commencing the annual festivities and the lively song honoring the deceased. The reference to Aristotle clearly indicates that students in the Middle Ages found the Greek philosopher to be as dry and unpalatable as their modern counterparts. But this carol is just the opposite. Robust, uninhibited, and with an open taste for fun, "The Boar's Head Carol" is among the best carols from the premodern era, and one of its most enjoyable.

# Christmas Is Coming

The Christmas carol is a mass phenomenon. Year after year it is actively sung, played, or heard by diverse and varied segments of Western society. Because of this cultural pervasiveness, even the slightest of Christmastime songs can become annually recurring entities. Take, for example, the well-known English nursery rhyme, "Christmas is coming, the goose is getting fat; please put a penny in the old man's hat." As insubstantial and trivial as that ditty from about the eighteenth century may be, it still has developed into a carol of moderate popularity, and it has done so without being attached to a highly recognizable or especially attractive tune.

There have been several respectable melodies used with "Christmas Is Coming," including ones by English composers Edith Nesbit Bland (1858-1924) and Henry Walford Davies (1869-1941) and American composer Nick Reynolds (1933- ). The tune by Bland is perhaps the most successful, but none of these are exactly holiday classics, nor do they need to be. For as long as this folk round is set to an appropriate melody of some appeal, it will continue to be sung at Christmas because of its cheery charm and direct opportunity to participate in some lighthearted and uncomplicated holiday fun.

# Dance Carol

Dancing is definitely not the first association that most persons make with Christmas, and yet there is more than a modest affiliation between the two. Around the beginning of the modern era (roughly 1400) the carol involved as a popular dance form in reaction to the strictness and puritanism of the medieval period. There had been songs called carols prior to this development, but the carol really did not flourish until dancing became strongly intertwined with the music of Christmas during the fifteenth century or thereabouts. In fact, the word "carol" was probably derived from the Greek word "choros," meaning "dance."

A number of popular carols either have a dance rhythm or allude to dancing. "Good King Wenceslas," "Deck the Halls with Boughs of Holly," "Patapan," and "The Holly and the Ivy" all have quite danceable music, and "Ding Dong! Merrily on High" explicitly uses a folk dance tune. Among the carols which have dancing as a theme are "Tomorrow Shall Be My Dancing Day," "The Christmas Waltz," "Rockin' Around the Christmas Tree," and "Dance Carol" ("Nu är det Jul igen"), a Swedish folk song of the modern period. Also translated as "Christmas Is Here Again," "Christmas Has Come Again!," "Yuletide Is Here Again," and "Now It Is Christmastime," "Dance Carol" is the best-known carol from Sweden. The tune, indeed, is a national folk institution. The Hambo, a very popular folk dance, has traditionally been danced to the melody around the Christmas tree. For the Swedes, as well as other groups, dancing has enhanced the enjoyment of the holiday season.

# Deck the Halls with Boughs of Holly

If there is a carol which could be accurately categorized as totally uninhibited it would be "Deck the Halls with Boughs of Holly." Thoroughly and blatantly dedicated to frivolous merrymaking, with terminology such as "gay apparel," "merry measure," "joyous," and "heedless," plus the whimsical "Fa la la la la, la la la la" refrain, "Deck the Halls" is the classical model of the jolly secular carol. Reinforcing the lighthearted tone of the lyrics is the exquisitely vivacious yet solid and substantial melody which romps with free abandon throughout the decorated halls. With the absolute and unadulterated secularity of this great holiday song, one could easily conclude that it is antithetical to the religious nature of Christmas. There is no mention of Christmas and no hint of religious content. Yet it does have some indirect value for the sacred observance of the holiday. Its merry voice, zestful heart, and cheerful countenance, along with suggestions of purity of soul and innocence of disposition, all successfully augment the joyous and positive flow of the holiday.

The roundabout contribution of this highly secular song to the religious observance of the season is one of its decided ironies. Another of its ironies is the deep historical obscurity of this very familiar song. All that is known about the carol's background is its reputed origin in Wales. Presumably of folk creation, its date of origin is not at all certain and even the language in which the lyrics were first written is somewhat unsure. Most likely the original words were the English verses we now sing, but they could possibly have been Welsh. The compelling argument relating to linguistic background is the exceptional poetic rhythm of the English lyrics, which do not have the feel of a translation.

The dating of the song is difficult. The nonsense word repetition (Fa la la la la . . . ) is a popular device used in the Middle Ages. On the other hand, both words and music closely resemble songs of the

English Renaissance (sixteenth and early seventeenth centuries), particularly the madrigals that were so fashionable in sixteenth-century England. (It has been suggested, however, that because the first known printing of the lyrics was in New York in 1881, the words are of nineteenth-century American origin. This is hard to believe, for if such is the case, the author had to perform an amazingly artful and sophisticated feat of imitation.) We do know that by the eighteenth century the melody had traveled far enough to have been used by the great master Wolfgang Amadeus Mozart (1756-1791) in a duet for violin and piano. Overall, the few clues in the carol's history and style suggest that the most reasonable conjecture as to date is the sixteenth century. If so, this dynamic and very esthetic song would be a chronological cousin of Queen Elizabeth I and William Shakespeare, and would fit extremely well into that very energetic and productive era.

# Gloucestershire Wassail

The word wassail has several associated meanings. It is a salutation wishing health to a person, the festive activity surrounding the
merry salutation, and the alcoholic beverage used in the salutation
and festivities, especially spiced ale. With any or all of these defini-
tions in force on a given occasion, it is quite certain that the participants are happily involved with boisterous holiday revel.

There are two famous English Christmas songs using the term
wassail. The most popular one, "Wassail Song" ("Here We Come
A-Wassailing"), is misleadingly named since the intent of the song
is to portray the activities of carolers. (It should be noted that
wassail at one time also meant a song sung during the drinking
festivities.) Far more compatible with the wassail theme is "Gloucestershire Wassail," which is also known under the titles "Wassail,
Wassail All Over the Town," "Gloucestershire Wassailer's Song,"
and "Wassail Song." This eighteenth-century folk carol from the
Gloucestershire region of England is an open and direct celebration
of the most secular functions of the holiday season. It is a very
skillfully crafted tribute to the raucous rituals of Christmas cheer,
with a strong melody which is eminently suitable to the liveliness of
the occasion. And this type of song was by no means confined to
Gloucestershire. A carol with similar lyrics but a lesser tune ("Somerset Wassail" or "Wassail and Wassail All Over the Town!") was
created in the county of Somerset at about the same time. The
existence of multiple wassail songs illustrates the widespread popularity of the traditional wassail custom.

# Good King Wenceslas

Yes, there really was a ruler named Wenceslas. He was not a king but instead a duke of Bohemia in the tenth century, and his name in Czech was actually Vaclav. On the other hand, the description of him as "good" is completely justified. He was noted for his piety and devotion to the strengthening of Christianity in Bohemia. In 929 his brother Boleslav, who cannot be characterized as good, assassinated Vaclav and succeeded him as duke. By the eleventh century Vaclav was honored as the patron saint of Bohemia, thus allowing Vaclav in a historical sense to have the last laugh on his power-hungry brother.

In the thirteenth century a delightful tune was created someplace in Europe, quite possibly in Scandinavia or another northern part of that continent. In the sixteenth century (1582), the sprightly melody was published in the carol collection *Piae Cantiones*, accompanied by a spring carol called "Tempus adest floridum" ("Spring Has Now Unwrapped the Flowers"). In the nineteenth century, Englishman John Mason Neale (1818-1866) discovered the tune and in 1853 affixed to it some lyrics based on the story of Wenceslas. By that time the historical Bohemian personage had acquired an entourage of legends. Among these legends was the one about the poor man and the page which Neale wove into a carol. But Neale's skill at weaving was rather faulty, for the lyrics of "Wenceslas" are, quite honestly, on the horrible side, and have even received negative epithets such as "doggerel." Two other carols conceived by Neale at about the same time, "O Come, O Come Emmanuel" (1851) and "Good Christian Men, Rejoice" (1853), were, fortunately, better blessed literarily.

The seven-centuries-old tune, in contrast, is a bit of a marvel of both longevity and musical content. Its flowing spirit belies our usual but largely mistaken impressions that all of the Middle Ages were dull, uncreative, and culturally confining. In addition to its attachment to the flower song, its compelling attractiveness has also caused its linkage with the 1919 carol, "Gentle Mary Laid Her Child." The twentieth-century lyric, by Canadian Joseph Simpson Cook (1859-1933), is artistically superior to "Wenceslas" and is directly about Christmas. But "Wenceslas," despite its poor lyrics and its purely tangential connections to the holiday, will probably persevere over all rivals partly because of tradition and partly because of the perverse appeal of its good-natured narrative about feasting and suffering in the winter weather and, most of all, kindness. Although the lyrics, in their strange way, contribute to the song's success, the bouncy and festive melody is what really makes the carol a perennial favorite. No matter what the words may be, or whether the title is "Good King Wenceslas" or "Pious Duke Vaclav," just about anything associated with the tune will probably emerge a winner.

# Tomorrow Shall Be My Dancing Day

The sixteenth century, with perennial favorites such as "The First Nowell," "We Wish You a Merry Christmas," "God Rest You Merry, Gentlemen," "Deck the Halls with Boughs of Holly," Luther's "From Heaven Above to Earth I Come," and possibly "O Christmas Tree," is arguably the number one era in the long history of Christmas carols. The West Country of England, with folk songs such as "We Wish You a Merry Christmas," "The Snow Lay on the Ground," "Gloucestershire Wassail," "The First Nowell," and "Tomorrow Shall Be My Dancing Day," is perhaps the most productive region of that talented nation which reigns supreme in the creation of carols.

Both the sixteenth century and the West Country come together in the case of "My Dancing Day." At least they are the primary suspects in the authorship of that bouncy but quite deceptive composition. From first glance it would seem that "My Dancing Day" is a jolly secular carol. However, in spite of the romantic light-headedness and frivolity of the first verse and chorus, most of the piece is essentially religious. In fact, sections two and three are not even about Christmas but deal with the more serious occasions of Lent, Passiontide, Easter, and Ascension. It really is a strange carol, with love allusions intermixed with the most austere topics. Overall, though, the blend of a buoyant tune and the curious contradictions of the lyrics make it an appealing addition to the holiday.

# THE CHRISTMAS TREE
# AND HOLIDAY DECORATIONS

## The Holly and the Ivy

On the cusp of the seventeenth and eighteenth centuries, that is, around 1700, there may have been a mysterious cloud of carol creativity hovering over France and England. Or it might have been simple coincidence that two or perhaps three of the most successful Christmas songs from these two cultures were composed on or about that date, and in the midst of an era when the creation of fine carols was extremely rare. "Patapan," the delightful French song, and "The Holly and the Ivy," the exquisite English folk song with possible connections with France, were most likely created at the junction of the two centuries. Add to this "The Twelve Days of Christmas," the imaginative English folk carol, which may have affiliations with France and which dates by best guess from roughly the same time, and the case for the cloud does not seem quite so ludicrous. Factor into this the atypical or offbeat natures of all three excellent carols, plus their high degree of musical originality, and the cloud hypothesis becomes a little more believable.

Cloud or no, "The Holly and the Ivy" has one of the most celestially esthetic melodies of any carol. Possibly created in the Gloucestershire region (some authorities believe it originated in France), this highly allegorical song is one of the most popular carols in the international arena. Halfway around the world in Australia, another folk carol, "The Holly Bears a Berry," has been directly derived from the lyrics. This borrowing, it should be noted, is not unusual in the history of "The Holly and the Ivy," for in spite of the strangeness of the words to us today, the theme in the carol is far from unique.

During the medieval period in England, there were a number of songs mentioning the relationship between holly and ivy. The symbolism is one of rivalry between the male holly and the female ivy. Although this rivalry of the sexes is just as strong today, we in the twentieth century tend to overlook the original meaning of the lyrics and instead appreciate the holly and the ivy as holiday decorations. Our treatment of these symbols as objects attractive to the eye, furthermore, is entirely consistent with our treatment of the music as being attractive to the ear.

# It's Beginning to Look Like Christmas

The world has witnessed numerous accomplished men of music, but it only has produced one famous "Music Man." That outstanding 1957 musical by Meredith Willson (1902-1984), with its story of River City and rousing centerpiece "76 Trombones," is the principal component of fame for the accomplished man of music who created it. His artistic achievements, though, go much farther than that successful theatrical enterprise. In his earlier days, for example, he played with the Sousa band and was a fixture for awhile on the old George Burns and Gracie Allen radio show. After *The Music Man* another long-running Broadway show with both words and music by Willson was *The Unsinkable Molly Brown* (1960). In addition, he composed several well-remembered popular songs including "May the Good Lord Bless and Keep You" (1950) and the 1951 carol "It's Beginning to Look Like Christmas."

Willson's carol is a very pleasant and soothing description of holiday decorations, a topic not often covered by Christmas pieces. The tone of the song, then, goes together well with the similar qualities of the voice of Bing Crosby, who recorded it in 1951 and thereby added it to his most-impressive Christmas repertory. The song's connection to popular American holiday phenomena continued in 1963 when "It's Beginning to Look Like Christmas" was reused as a main theme in Willson's Christmas musical *Here's Love*, which had some success. That production was based on the classic 1947 movie *Miracle on 34th Street*, which, like Willson's carol, appears to be a permanent fixture of the holiday season.

# O Christmas Tree

When the saintly medieval carols go marching into musical heaven, "O Tannenbaum" will not be in their number. For in spite of widespread belief to the contrary, that German folk piece is almost surely not from the Middle Ages. The myth probably developed because the carol's origins are unclear and because the original German words are quite simple in style and content. This combination of obscurity and patent simplicity apparently led to the almost universal opinion that the carol must be from an older, less-complex era, that is, the medieval period.

But three factors refute the alleged medieval creation of the song. First, the style of the excellent melody suggests early modern composition. Everything about the music smacks of the Renaissance or soon after. Second, only the first verse of the lyrics is from the folk domain. Stanzas two and three are by the German poet Ernst Gebhard Anschütz (1800-1861). Completion of the lyrics in the nineteenth century implies that the first verse has some degree of chronological closeness to the later time. Third, the Christmas tree was not a popular holiday institution until after the Protestant Reformation of the sixteenth century. Therefore, it is unlikely that a song glorifying the December evergreen would have been written before then.

By all indications, the most plausible time of composition was the sixteenth or seventeenth century. A later time could be inferred from the dates of the first publication of the music (1799) and words (1820), but a post-seventeenth century dating does not feel right. One thing that is much more certain is that the melody had traversed the Atlantic Ocean by the nineteenth century and in 1861 was adapted for "Maryland, My Maryland." The lyrics, however, probably would not have even traveled outside of its immediate local area of composition (which possibly could have been Westphalia) without being attached to the stimulating and vital tune. More than any other well-known carol, the melody supports the continued survival of the carol. The German words are far from great, although the song is very popular in Germany, and it is quite difficult to translate them into English without the words ending up trite or even outright stupid-sounding. There have been a number of translations tried, but none of them have been able to convert inferiority to superiority. Several English versions have appeared under the title "O Christmas Tree," and, in addition, "The Christmas Tree," "O Christmas Pine," "Oh Tree of Fir," and others have been utilized. However, the consistent result, in varying degrees, has been a set of lyrics widely separated in artistic quality from the exceptional melody. Of all the more famous songs of the Christmas season, none other has as broad a chasm between its two components.

# Rockin' Around the Christmas Tree

With the very notable exception of "O Tannenbaum" ("O Christmas Tree"), there are surprisingly few carols which emphasize the widely shared experience of a decorated Christmas tree. "Du gronne, glitrende tre, god-dag!" ("You Green and Glittering Tree, Good Day!") from Denmark, "Am Weihnachtsbaum die Lichter brennen" ("The Christmas Tree with Its Candles Gleaming") from Germany, and "Christopher the Christmas Tree," "Do You Know How Christmas Trees Are Grown?," "Gather Around the Christmas Tree," and "Rockin' Around the Christmas Tree" from the United States also are based on this theme. Of all these songs, only "Tannenbaum" is especially well known, with "Gather Around" (by John Henry Hopkins [1820-1891], the composer of "We Three Kings of Orient Are") and "Rockin'" (by Johnny Marks [1909-1985]) being of secondary importance. On top of belonging to the rare breed of Christmas tree carols, "Rockin'," published in 1958, is one of the relatively few good carols written using the medium of rock music. "Jingle Bell Rock" (1957), by Joseph Beal (1900- ) and James Boothe (1917- ) is perhaps the only other one of note. The association of "Rockin'" with underpopulated categories, though, is limited to the two aspects indicated above. Its author, Marks, has "Rudolph the Red-Nosed Reindeer" and a number of other songs to his credit including "A Holly Jolly Christmas" (1962), "Jingle, Jingle, Jingle" (1964), "Silver and Gold" (1964), "The Most Wonderful Day of the Year" (1964), "When Santa Claus Gets Your Letter" (1950), "A Caroling We Go" (1966), a 1952 musical setting for "'Twas the Night Before Christmas," and a variant tune for Longfellow's "I Heard the Bells on Christmas Day." He may well be the most successful American popular composer of all time, possibly even surpassing Irving Berlin and his two Christmas contributions, "Happy Holiday" and "White Christmas."

# CAROLING

## Caroling, Caroling

Most typically, Christmas songs which became successful among twentieth-century American audiences are launched via the mass media. The high exposure of radio, television, and motion pictures is extremely valuable for catching the attention of the public. Yet there is a recent American carol which did not have the advantage of such media promotion, nor did it have the benefit of presentation in a hymnal or other important church publication, nor was it associated with a familiar or established name. Despite these obstacles, "Caroling, Caroling" has been slowly but progressively working its way into the American holiday season.

"Caroling, Caroling" is the best-known song of the body of 15 carols collectively called the "Alfred Burt Carols." They were named after the composer of the music, Alfred S. Burt (1919 or 1920-1954), who died at the extremely young age of 34. Burt, who was obscure at the time of the publication of his carols (1954), still remains obscure today in spite of the increasing success of "Caroling, Caroling" and some of his other carols such as "Some Children See Him" and "The Star Carol." The lyricists for the Alfred Burt carols were Wihla Hutson, who wrote the verses for the three songs mentioned above as well as others, and Burt's minister father, Bates Gilbert Burt (1878-1948). Originally written for children, and as annual Christmas gifts, the carols tend to be religious in content and simple and inhibited in style.

Among recent carols dealing with the theme of Christmas singing, "Caroling, Caroling" is perhaps the leading example, but "A

Caroling We Go," composed in 1966 by Johnny Marks of "Rudolph the Red-Nosed Reindeer" fame, may also vie for that distinction. Altogether, the Alfred Burt Carols comprise one of the most significant bodies of holiday songs ever produced by one artist. They perhaps may never become highly familiar international favorites. But they have sufficient esthetic merit and have gained sufficient public attention to have been honored by the performance of a medley by the superlative Boston Pops Orchestra.

# Fum, Fum, Fum

The Catalonia region of northeast Spain (the area about the city of Barcelona), has long had strong affinities with the nearby regions of France, especially with the southern French area of Provence. Because of this, Catalonia has developed a language and culture distinctly different from much of the rest of Spain. Catalan literature is second in importance only to Spanish, and the history of the region is robustly recurrent with themes of independence and autonomy. Among its other characteristics, the region's civilization is noted for possibly being the leading producer of carols on the Iberian Peninsula. This phenomenon is no accident, for its culturally kindred French region of Provence is also an exceptional source of Christmas songs.

Although no carol from Spain has really developed into a world-class song, several carols from Catalonia have gained a degree of international recognition. These include the folk songs "El cant dels ocells" ("Carol of the Birds"), "El desembre congelat" ("The Icy December"), and "Fum, Fum, Fum," arguably the most famous Spanish carol. The last song is most commonly translated under the same nonsense-word title "Fum, Fum, Fum" or else the similar "Foom, Foom, Foom." It is uncertain when the carol was written, but the best guess perhaps is the Spanish Renaissance or Golden Age (the sixteenth and seventeenth centuries). With its joyous exhortation to proclaim Christmas in song as expressed in the opening line of one of its English translations, "On this joyful Christmas Day sing Fum, Fum, Fum," it appears to be a product of that lively period of Spanish civilization. Since it is quite possibly the best of the Spanish carols, it could most suitably be dubbed "the Golden Carol from the Golden Age."

# On Christmas Night

The English have a curious custom of naming some of their folk carols after the places of their supposed origin. Among the recipients of this process are "Somerset Carol," "Somerset Wassail," "Gloucestershire Wassail," and "Coventry Carol." In contrast, other cultures do not ordinarily designate their carols in a similar manner. There are no such things as "Provençal Carol," "Catalan Carol," or "Kentucky Carol."

This somewhat unique practice is just one small facet of a centuries-old English attachment to and passion for the Christmas carol. The tradition of identifying areas of English turf with certain carols implies a special degree of intimacy with the genre at which they so exceedingly excel. No other nation even comes close to the carol accomplishments of that island nation which has, ironically, been sometimes regarded as unmusical. So when they designate the very good folk carol "On Christmas Night" as "Sussex Carol," it must be interpreted as an offshoot of their long-term involvement with the esthetic tones of Christmas. It is yet another manifestation of the English propensity to thoroughly observe the holiday with music. Or, as the words of the possibly eighteenth-century song happily announce, "On Christmas night all Christians sing."

# Sing We Now of Christmas

In the Middle Ages the Provence region of southern France was famous for its wandering troubadours. Another exceptional musical tradition from Provence is its considerable contribution to Christmas carol literature. From that culturally unique region have come four of the better-known Christmas songs, "La marche des rois" ("The March of Kings"), "Un flambeau, Jeannette, Isabelle" ("Bring a Torch, Jeannette, Isabella"), the lyrics for "Cantique de Noël ("O Holy Night"), and "Noël nouvelet" ("Sing We Now of Christmas").

Also known under the English titles "Christmas Comes Anew," "Nowell, Sing Nowell," and "Noel! A New Noel!," "Sing We Now" is a seventeenth- or eighteenth-century folk song. In the style and spirit of the medieval troubadours, it is a declaration that the singers are enjoying their celebration of the holiday. The positive spirit of the music has led to the adaptation of the melody for some hymns and also for the organ composition "Variations sur un vieux noël" ("Variations on an Old Carol") by the French classical composer Marcel Dupré (1886-1971). Note that Dupré described the relatively recent song as an "old carol." From the parochial viewpoint of the twentieth century it perhaps could be regarded as old, but what then do we call a song such as "The March of the Kings," which was created four or five hundred years prior to "Sing We Now of Christmas"?

# Wassail Song

Few holiday songs equal or surpass the liveliness, vivaciousness, and sparkling gaiety of the seventeenth-century carol "Wassail Song." This folk creation from the Yorkshire region of England is also known under the titles "Here We Come A-Wassailing," "Here We Come A-Caroling," and "Here We Go A-Caroling." Since the wassail is a drinking custom, and the basic purpose of the song is to describe carolers going from door to door (no doubt encouraged by an occasional wassail), the titles with the word "caroling" are more appropriate to the theme than are the titles with the word wassail.

This convivial song has several jovial relatives. Two verses of the carol have been treated as a separate song, "Good-Bye," or "God Bless the Master of This House," with the same exceptional tune utilized. A carol with similar words but a different tune is "We've Been a While Awandering," probably of the same century and region as "Wassail Song." The most famous relative is "Gloucestershire Wassail" ("Wassail, Wassail All Over the Town"), an eighteenth-century folk song from Gloucestershire, England. This later carol, which sports an unabashed invitation to partake of festivities throughout the community, is truly deserving of the "wassail" terminology.

"Wassail Song," with its friendly and well-crafted lyrics and its excellent melody, is one of the finest expressions of the secular celebration of the holiday season. No other Christmas song has approached its ability to represent the joy of caroling. The personalness of the verses and the energy of the tune unite to provide warmth to the carolers going about in the cold winter weather.

# We Sing in Celebration

Some songs are most noted for their longstanding popularity. Other songs are most noted for their influence on similar compositions. "We Sing in Celebration," a fifteenth-century French carol, belongs a bit in both categories. A fair amount of twentieth-century collections contain the song in one form or another, and so it can lay claim to a certain degree of longstanding fame. An unusual number of other carols have been derived from this song, and so it can also claim considerable cultural influence. Only one other carol, the fourteenth-century song "Puer natus in Bethlehem" ("A Boy Is Born in Bethlehem"), exceeds "We Sing in Celebration" in the number of borrowings by carols.

The borrowed element in "We Sing" is its attractive folk tune. That traveling melody has been utilized in at least five carols, plus a number of other songs, both secular and sacred. Which set of lyrics it was initially attached to is uncertain. It may have been "Célébrons la naissance," an anonymous fifteenth-century French text from which the translation for "We Sing" was extracted. (Other translations of "Célébrons" are "We Celebrate the Birth" and "O Publish the Glad Story.") Or it may have been "Chantons! Je vous prie," a French lyric by Lucas Le Moigne who lived in the first half of the fifteenth century. (Among the translations of "Chantons!" are "Now Sing We All Full Sweetly" and "Now Let Us Sing, I Pray.")

All of the above titles touch upon the theme of Christmas singing, but the melody's matching with other poetic topics has been common and facile. Within the limits of meter and length of lines, the tune has served as sort of an all-purpose musical part. This exceptional versatility testifies to the enduring quality of this unpretentious old folk melody.

# CHRISTMAS BELLS

## Carol of the Bells

The Ukraine region of the former Soviet Union has been frequently misunderstood. Although for centuries it was more than large enough to be an independent medium-sized nation, which it now is, and had a language, alphabet, and culture distinct from the dominant Russians, the Ukrainians were often mistakenly labeled "Russians." This miscomprehension affected all sectors of their civilization, including the one famous contribution to the literature of carols to emanate from the Ukraine.

The music for the very popular holiday song, "Carol of the Bells," was created by the Ukraine's most popular composer, Mykola Dmytrovich Leontovych (1877-1921). Despite being born in Ukraine, living in Ukraine, and largely working with Ukrainian music, Leontovych and his works are more than occasionally called "Russian." The composition from which "Carol of the Bells" was derived, the choral work *Shchedryk*, which was first performed by students at Kiev University in December 1916, has not been exempted from the mislabeling. But the Ukrainians, from one perspective, have had the last laugh in this cultural comedy of errors, for by far the best-known carol music to originate in any portion of the former Soviet Union was Leontovych's brilliant musical portrayal of the sounds of Christmas bells.

Only 20 years after its composition, the music from *Shchedryk* was converted into a carol halfway around the world. Peter J. Wilhousky (1902-1978), a composer, lyricist, and conductor who worked with Arturo Toscanini on NBC radio, adapted Leontovych's music and added some lyrics. The title chosen by New Jerseyite Wilhousky was ideal, for "Carol of the Bells" is not only extremely suitable as a characterization of the melody, but also is completely harmonious with the old Slavic legend on which *Shchedryk* is based. At midnight on the night Jesus was born, the legend claims, every bell in the world rang out in his honor.

Since the synthesis of "Carol of the Bells" in 1936, the song, also known as "Ukrainian Carol," has increasingly become a part of the celebration of Christmas in the United States. Its public acceptance was surely boosted by the employment of the melody in a series of television advertisements for champagne. The idea, apparently, was that the champagne was as tasteful and sparkling as the music. In addition, the melody has been utilized in three other American carols. In 1947, M. L. Holman wrote "Ring, Christmas Bells." In 1957, the anonymous lyrics "Come, Dance and Sing" were published, and by 1972 another "Carol of the Bells" (this time anonymous) was published. Wilhousky's original "Carol of the Bells" can be easily distinguished from the later one by his first line, "Hark! How the bells, sweet silver bells." The second "Carol of the Bells" starts with "Hark to the bells, Hark to the bells." This multiple usage of Leontovich's music for four carols as well as for a variety of other purposes is sound testimony to its quality and popular appeal.

# Ding Dong! Merrily on High

During the late sixteenth century, the first productions which resemble modern ballet began to be presented. Completely consistent with this development, the first treatise on ballet dancing was published at about the same time. Entitled *Orchésographie*, the landmark 1588 volume by Frenchman Thoinot Arbeau (1519-1595) also has a small niche in the history of carols. Arbeau's book was probably the first publication to include the gentle sixteenth-century French folk melody which is now used for the carol "Ding Dong! Merrily on High."

Three centuries or so after it appeared in *Orchésographie*, the old folk tune, called "Branle de l'officiel" ("The Dance of the Official"), was attached to a set of lyrics which resembled the poetry of early modern England. It can be inferred that their author, Englishman George Ratcliffe Woodward (1848-1934), deliberately intended that his verses fit in with the Renaissance style of the melody. This practice was a consistent pattern for Woodward, who also wrote the old-sounding carols "Hail! Blessed Virgin Mary!," "O the Morn, the Merry, Merry, Morn," and "Our Lady Sat within Her Bower," all coupled with sixteenth- or seventeenth-century tunes. On top of creating lyrics, Woodward also translated a number of carols and compiled three significant collections. All of his work tended to be with older carols. Apparently, his body was in the twentieth century, but his artistic soul was rooted in earlier times. If this had not been so, the softly lyrical "Ding Dong! Merrily on High" would never have graced our Christmases.

# I Heard the Bells on Christmas Day

In spite of the mentions of bells and Christmas in the title, "I Heard the Bells on Christmas Day" is as much an antiwar song as it is a pro-Christmas song. The poetry of this renowned carol was crafted by the great American literary figure, Henry Wadsworth Longfellow (1807-1882), in the midst of the American Civil War. On Christmas Day in 1863, Longfellow wrote the familiar lines in response to the horror of the bloody fratricidal conflict in general and to the personal tragedy of his son, Lieutenant Charles Appleton Longfellow, who was severely wounded in November 1862.

This was not the only pacifist poetry composed by Longfellow. His peace sentiments found their way into many poems, including the famous "Song of Hiawatha" (1855) and "Courtship of Miles Standish" (1858). Although his reputation rests primarily on his considerable skill as a popular poet, which also resulted in the well-known works "The Village Blacksmith," (1841), "The Wreck of the Hesperus" (1841), "Evangeline" (1847), and "Paul Revere's Ride" (1863), his deep-rooted pacifism, as well as his concern with social issues such as slavery, should not be overlooked in the understanding of the man.

It was not until sometime after 1872 that the 1863 poem, which was originally titled "Christmas Bells," was converted into a carol. Some unknown person in some unknown year recognized that Longfellow's stirring and optimistic interpretation of the bells of Christmas would make a magnificent mate for an 1872 processional which was strongly reminiscent of the ringing of bells. The composer of the appropriate tune, John Baptiste Calkin (1827-1905), was the most famous of a family of accomplished English musicians. At first Calkin's melody was published with the 1848 American hymn, "Fling Out the Banner! Let It Float" by George Washington Doane (1799-1859). Ironically, "Fling Out" was an old-fashioned militant missionary hymn which contrasted greatly in purpose and spirit from the more permanent partner of Calkin's music, "I Heard the Bells."

Although Calkin's melody is a beautiful, gentle, and lofty rendition of the sounds of Christmas bells and is quite well received during the holidays, at least three alternative tunes have been tried. These are the moderately popular wafting melody by Johnny Marks (1909-1985), who is most noted for "Rudolph the Red-Nosed Reindeer," plus tunes by John Bishop (ca. 1665-1737) and Alfred Herbert Brewer (1865-1928). Calkin's melody, however, remains predominant over the others.

As a pair, the resonant tones of Calkin's pensive music, the main component of his reputation, and the minor but excellent poem by Longfellow, comprise a very satisfying carol. On top of its fine artistry, it offers an undeniable moral whose essence resides in the two phrases with which each stanza ends. "Peace on earth, goodwill to men" so appropriately covers both halves of the partly Christmas and partly pacifist carol. No matter how long this particular song may endure, may its two highly desirable themes harmoniously blend together in an everlasting symbiosis for the benefit of humanity.

# Jingle Bell Rock

Was it coincidence or was it deliberate? That inquiry jumps out during a review of the history of "Jingle Bell Rock." Written in 1957, during the earlier and saner period of rock music, "Jingle Bell Rock" was introduced to the ear of the public exactly one hundred years after the creation of "Jingle Bells." Whether accident or plan, the composition of a follow-up song on the centennial of the earlier piece was an ideal public relations move.

The backgrounds of "Jingle Bell Rock" 's creators are strongly suggestive that the song was specifically designed to take advantage of the special anniversary. Massachusetts-born Joseph Carleton Beal (1900- ) and Texas-born James R. Boothe (1917- ), who collaborated on the words and music, were both in the publicity business. Beal was deeply involved with public relations activities, and Boothe was associated with newspaper reporting and advertising copywriting. But any initial boost given by publicity would not have sustained the song if it did not have a certain amount of intrinsic appeal. As is unfortunately so pervasive throughout rock music, the words defy any precise interpretation. The melody, on the other hand, is in some vague, indefinable way fairly attractive and even slightly resembles a passage from Act I of Tchaikovsky's immortal 1877 ballet, *Swan Lake*. Just as important, it manages to sustain itself in repetition year after year. The lighthearted, inoffensive, pleasant qualities of "Jingle Bell Rock" have probably made it the most successful of rock Christmas songs. It demonstrates that at least occasionally the sentiments of Christmas and the style of rock music can be compatible.

# Jingle Bells

"Jingle Bells" and "We Three Kings of Orient Are" have much in common as historical phenomena. They both are American carols created in 1857. ("Bells" was probably composed in Boston and "Kings" probably in New York City.) They both were written for children. ("Bells" was created for a Sunday school program and "Kings" for the author's nephews and nieces.) Only one person was responsible for both words and music in each case. For "Bells" it was the Boston-born popular composer James S. Pierpont (1822-1893), and for "Kings" it was John Henry Hopkins (1820-1891). As if these coincidences were not enough, both Pierpont and Hopkins lived to approximately 71 years of age.

Artistically, though, the two songs have nothing in common except the use of the English language and the Christmas holiday they both enhance. "Kings" is smooth in style, oriental in atmosphere, biblical in content, and religious in purpose. "Bells" is bouncy in style, folksy in atmosphere, contemporary in content, and secular in purpose. Even the geographical environments are drastically dissimilar, with "Kings" enacted in a warm, dry climate and "Bells" in the winter season of a northern climate. On top of all this, "Kings" is deeply involved with the Christmas story while "Bells" does not in any manner mention or hint of the December holiday.

Another historical curiosity is that "Kings" is often regarded as old, while "Bells" is often regarded as recent. These misperceptions, however, are quite understandable in light of the radically contrasting spirits and forms of the two highly popular carols. Another understandable misimpression is the sometimes attribution of "Bells" to Connecticut-born lyricist John Pierpont (1785-1866), since the text of the carol is usually identified only by the name "J. Pierpont." Other debatable areas relating to "Bells" are whether it was the first well-known American secular carol, and whether it is the most popular American secular carol today. The first matter is the easiest. "Bells" was probably the first secular carol of consequence in the United States, although "Up on the Housetop," which was composed in the 1850s or 1860s, could have preceded it. Another secular carol which could possibly be earlier than "Bells" is the anonymous and undated song, "Jolly Old Saint Nicholas." The odds are, though, that "Nicholas" is somewhat later.

The second debatable matter is much more complex. There is some opinion that "White Christmas" is more popular than "Jingle Bells." Certainly it can be argued that "White Christmas" has become extremely popular since its premiere only two generations ago in 1942. Yet when frequency of performance, familiarity to all sectors of society, and position in the culture of Christmas are closely analyzed, it would appear that at least for the moment "Jingle Bells" is still number one. If for no other reason, "Jingle Bells" remains on top because of longevity. But either way, "Jingle Bells" is a highly enjoyable song which is the stereotypical symbol of the secular observance of the holiday. It is so lively and happy that the carol participant can become fully involved in the sensation of riding, as Pierpont's original title proclaims, in a deliciously invigorating "One Horse Open Sleigh."

For a different set of lyrics for Pierpont's tune, try this:

## The Christmas Grouch

Verse:     December twenty-four
           Is knocking at the door
           I can't believe it's here
           What happened to the year?
           The recent weeks have flown
           As fast as ever known
           Yet now the days begin to drag
           My spirits soon will sag.

Refrain:   Ouch, ouch, ouch
           Christmas grouch
           Shopping go away
           Oh what pain
           What mental strain
           On ev'ry holiday

Ouch, ouch, ouch
Christmas grouch
Lots more bills to pay
Oh what pain
What mental strain
On ev'ry holiday.

Verse:    December twenty-five
Is begging to arrive
The snow is getting deep
Oh let me go to sleep!
There's reindeer on the roof
With noisy sled and hoof
And soon that pesky annual elf
Will manifest himself.

Refrain:    Ouch, ouch, ouch
Christmas grouch
Santa go away
Oh what pain
What mental strain
On ev'ry holiday
Ouch, ouch, ouch
Christmas grouch
Blast that silly sleigh
Oh what pain
What mental strain
On ev'ry holiday.

Verse:    December twenty-six
Has got me in a fix
The place is such a mess
I'll run away, I guess
This time is such a curse
None other could be worse
It's s'pposed to be a lot of fun
But not for ev'ryone.

Refrain:     Ouch, ouch, ouch
             Christmas grouch
             Headache go away
             Oh what pain
             What mental strain
             On ev'ry holiday
             Ouch, ouch, ouch
             Christmas grouch
             Such an awful day
             Oh what pain
             What mental strain
             On ev'ry holiday.

                              –William Studwell

# Silver Bells

London-born Leslie Townes Hope (1903- ), better known as Bob Hope, has done far more than his share to entertain Americans via radio, television, movies, and war-zone shows. Among his numerous achievements was the introduction of the Christmas ballad "Silver Bells" in the 1951 holiday movie, *The Lemon Drop Kid*. In duet with actress Marilyn Maxwell, Hope brought this graceful, sentimental piece about Christmas in the city to the attention of millions of movie-goers.

Only a generation or so later "Silver Bells" has become a familiar standard, perhaps even a classic, of the Christmas season. Assembled by two talented popular artists, lyricist Ray Evans (1915- ) and musician Jay Livingston (1915- ), "Silver Bells" combines a contemporary urban setting with old-fashioned emotional responses. This skillful blend is the essence of the song's continued prosperity.

Ray, from New York State, and Jay, from Pennsylvania, also collaborated on other successful compositions, including three Academy Award winners, "Buttons and Bows" (1948), "Mona Lisa" (1950), and "Whatever Will Be, Will Be" or "Que Sera, Sera" (1956). "Silver Bells" did not win any kind of award, but if there were an honors category for popular Christmas songs, the silver-toned piece from the movie with the funny name would probably capture one of the highest places in the competition.

# SANTA CLAUS

## Here Comes Santa Claus

You cannot find it in an atlas, dictionary, or gazetteer. Only Santa Claus and his associates, plus those who watch Santa go down "Santa Claus Lane" in Los Angeles' Christmas parade, plus all the children of the world, know where Santa Claus Lane is. The rest of us have been annually reminded that it indeed does exist since the song "Here Comes Santa Claus (Right down Santa Claus Lane)" made its debut in 1946.

Written by Texan Orvon Gene Autry (1907- ), movie actor, singer, composer, media executive, and baseball team owner, in collaboration with Oakley Haldeman (1909- ), a composer and music publisher from California, this simple song has been especially popular with children over the years. Autry himself increased the popularity of the piece by singing the most successful recorded version. Later on, Autry collaborated on another Christmas song, "Nestor, the Long-Eared Christmas Donkey," written in 1975 with Don Pfrimmer and Dave Burgess. "Nestor" did not have the magic of "Here Comes Santa Claus" or of Autry's fantastically well-received 1949 recording of "Rudolph the Red-Nosed Reindeer." Obviously, it was hoped that Nestor, who like Rudolph had a much-maligned physical abnormality, would be adopted to a similar degree by the American public. But "Nestor" was missing one ingredient which was strongly present in Autry's two other Christmas efforts. While Rudolph guided the sleigh through fog in 1949 and Santa drove down an imaginary lane in 1946, Nestor had no such geographical advantage.

# I Saw Mommy Kissing Santa Claus

Was it really Daddy in the Santa Claus suit, or was the boy who saw Mommy kissing Santa Claus underneath the mistletoe a silent witness to a holiday soap opera love triangle? Only Mommy, the man in the Santa Claus suit, and Tommie Connor know for sure. Connor, who is not well known for anything else, wrote the words and music to this very popular American holiday diversion in 1952.

Part of what made the song such a success was the engaging recording made by Jimmy Boyd, who handled the role of the unsuspecting youth in a most believable fashion. Without the required touch of naïveté, Connor's song would probably not have done so well. Although the lyrics are cute, the melody is on the weak side, and only an exceptional recording would have delivered it into our December affections and kept it there on a long-term basis.

# Jolly Old Saint Nicholas

In addition to being a bright and lively Christmas song, "Jolly Old Saint Nicholas" is somewhat unique. It is the only highly popular American carol, with the exception of black spirituals, which has no attribution of authorship. Its style and content indicate probable composition in the second half of the nineteenth century or possibly very early in the twentieth, but no name has ever been associated with this delightful piece.

Yet the story does not necessarily end there. At about the same time that "Jolly Old Saint Nicholas" was created, another carol of similar style and content was composed. This other song was "Up on the Housetop," written in the 1850s or 1860s by Benjamin R. Hanby (1833-1867). The melodies of both pieces have similar rhythm and mood. Both sets of lyrics, furthermore, contain references to Nell or Nellie and use both Santa Claus plus Saint Nick or Saint Nicholas to designate that jolly altruistic character. Add to these patterns the obscureness of Hanby and the sometimes attribution of "Up on the Housetop" to "traditional," and the result is a case, admittedly very weak and tenuous, for authorship by Hanby. If Hanby did not write "Jolly Old Saint Nicholas," then whoever did may have been affected by Hanby's artistic style.

# Santa Claus Is Comin' to Town

Two elements in this song have made it of particular interest to children as well as adults. First is the attention-getting opening-line warning, "You better watch out," and second is the delightful promise of an upcoming event, "Santa Claus is comin' to town." Coupled with a bouncy and catchy melody, these teasers have made the 1932 composition by lyricist Haven Gillespie (1888-1975) and musician John Frederick Coots (1897- ) one of the most successful of all American popular Christmas carols. Only "Rudolph" and "White Christmas" have outsold this depression-era joyful gem.

"Santa Claus Is Comin'" was the best-known piece by either Gillespie or Coots, although Kentuckian Gillespie also produced a number of good songs including "That Lucky Old Sun" (1949) and Brooklyn-born Coots included in his successes the romantic ballad "Love Letters in the Sand" (1931). It was only by luck and/or persistence that their famous collaborative achievement ever got recorded. Two frustrating years passed before the songwriters could get anyone to sing their composition. Finally, just before Thanksgiving 1934, Eddie Cantor, the popular entertainer and Coot's employer, performed the song on his radio show. (It took some persuasion from Cantor's wife Ida to bring about the premiere.) Needless to say, Cantor's presentation was extremely well received, and "Santa Claus Is Comin'," aided by subsequent multimillion-selling recordings by Bing Crosby with the Andrews Sisters and by Perry Como, has become one of the more pleasant fixtures of our holiday season.

The song also has a special historical significance. It was the first in a series of top Christmas songs to appear during a uniquely productive generation from 1932 to 1951. The inhabitants of this consequential period include "I Wonder As I Wander," "Winter Wonderland," "Carol of the Bells," "Happy Holiday," "White Christmas," "The Little Drummer Boy," "I'll Be Home for Christmas," "Have Yourself a Merry Little Christmas," "Let It Snow!

Let it Snow! Let It Snow!," "All I Want for Christmas Is My Two Front Teeth," "Here Comes Santa Claus," "The Christmas Song," "Sleigh Ride," "A Marshmallow World," "Rudolph the Red-Nosed Reindeer," "Frosty the Snowman," "Silver Bells," and "It's Beginning to Look Like Christmas." Nineteen holiday favorites in about the same number of years!

# 'Twas the Night Before Christmas

With the exception of Charles Dickens' incomparable 1843 masterpiece *A Christmas Carol*, no Christmas writing in the English language is as beloved or influential as the 1822 poem, "A Visit from St. Nicholas" or "'Twas the Night Before Christmas." Reportedly composed for an everyday, pragmatic reason–to please a sick son–the verses by New Yorker Clement Clarke Moore (1779-1863) have become a minor literary landmark of the United States. Although the legends of St. Nicholas had existed for centuries before, it was not until Moore took pen in hand that St. Nicholas, or the derivative name Santa Claus, took on the traits and role which we now identify with the character. In effect, then, Moore invented the modern myth of Santa Claus.

Possibly because it might be considered undignified for a professor of Oriental and Greek literature to dabble in such light pastimes, Moore first published his poem in a somewhat distant location–Troy, New York. It appeared in the *Troy Sentinel* on December 23, 1823. Although printed as a poem in countless publications since then, its first-known conversion to a song was in 1942. In that year Nebraskan Kenneth Lorin ("Ken") Darby (1909- ) an Oscar-winning composer, lyricist, and conductor who invented the Munchkin voices for the 1939 movie *The Wizard of Oz*, composed a musical setting for Moore's words. Soon after, two other composers followed suit. In 1951 Frank Henri Klickmann (1885-1966) wrote an accompanying tune, and in 1952 the ubiquitous Johnny Marks (1909-1985) contributed his melodic version. Of these three, Darby's was definitly the best. None of these tunes, however, has been particularly well received by the American public, and none of them was used in the 1974 television special, *'Twas the Night Before Christmas*, which was narrated by Joel Grey. Perhaps part of the problem is that only a highly exceptional melody will ever be regarded as worthy of Moore's much revered holiday classic.

# Up on the Housetop

"Up on the Housetop" may well have been the first American song of importance which elaborates on the theme of Santa Claus. It also is one of the first entirely secular Christmas songs composed in the United States. Written by little-known Benjamin R. Hanby (1833-1867), sometime in the 1850s or 1860s, and probably in Ohio, this vivacious song could possibly predate the early secular classic, "Jingle Bells" (1857). The best estimate, though, is that Hanby's song was created in the 1860s.

Hanby's life was short, less than 35 years. Yet he did manage to contribute this bouncy song, which is an especial favorite of children, to the enduring literature of the holiday. Furthermore, he may possibly have composed another popular carol, "Jolly Old Saint Nicholas," which is of roughly the same period and which has a suspiciously similar style of music and lyrics. There is absolutely no evidence that Hanby was responsible for the other song, yet the chronological and stylistic coincidences, plus the total anonymity of "Jolly Old Saint Nicholas," do elicit the conjecture that Hanby might have authored both songs. At the least, Hanby's "Up on the Housetop" may have influenced "Jolly Old Saint Nicholas."

# Just Because He's Santa Claus

In case you have not gotten your fill of silly Santa songs, try the following, an original 1991 melody by William Studwell. With some variations in the refrain, the song was recorded in 1994 by Hilltop Records, Hollywood, on audio cassette.

1. 'Round Christmas Day it always snows
   Why this occurs nobody knows
   But could it be, can it be true?
   I'll leave the answer up to you.

   Refrain (repeated):
   Winter follows nature's laws
   Just because he's Santa Claus
   Just because he's Santa, Santa, Santa Claus.

2. The stockings of good girls and boys
   Are always stuffed with lots of toys
   I can't explain why this should be
   But very, very possibly.

   Refrain (repeated):
   North Pole toy elves work their saws
   Just because he's Santa Claus
   Just because he's Santa, Santa, Santa Claus.

3. The Christmas sleigh is never late
   It gets there on the proper date
   Though nothing is completely clear
   I think all's due to eight small deer.

   Refrain (repeated):
   Tiny reindeer race their paws
   Just because he's Santa Claus
   Just because he's Santa, Santa, Santa Claus.

4. Oh, this is just an annual ruse
   A plot designed to help confuse
   As far as all the world can tell
   It spreads confusion very well.

   Refrain (repeated):
   Puzzled grownups always pause
   Just because he's Santa Claus
   Just because he's Santa, Santa, Santa Claus.

5. But in the end there's joy and glee
   Surrounding each bright Christmas tree
   With goodies piled of every sort
   For offspring a delightful sport.

   Refrain (repeated):
   Happy children give applause
   Just because he's Santa Claus
   Just because he's Santa, Santa, Santa Claus.

   –William Studwell

# CHRISTMAS ANIMALS

# Almost Day

Murder, assault, and jail terms are not the type of activities that are normally associated with the composition of Christmas carols. Yet all of these were part of the life of the popular black composer Huddie Ledbetter (1885-1949), also known as Leadbelly. He wandered through his native Louisiana and Texas, singing, playing the guitar, and sometimes getting into brawls. He was jailed three times for violent crimes, including murder and attempted murder.

Beneath the criminal facade, though, was an artist of considerable talent. Among the compositions by Ledbetter were "Good Night Irene" (1936), and the Christmas song "Almost Day" or "It's Almost Day." With the original opening line, "Chickens a-crow-in' for Midnight," the reference to a turkey, and the square-dance tempo, Ledbetter's song is one of the more interesting carols produced in the twentieth century. As with most of his songs, it is unknown exactly when "Almost Day" was created. The best guess might be the 1920s or 1930s, a period heavily marred by prison sojourns. During one of Ledbetter's stays in jail, in 1932, famous folklorist John Avery Lomax (1867-1948) recorded Ledbetter's compositions, thus preserving them for future generations. In the last decade of his life, Ledbetter performed in numerous nightclubs, and even toured France in his final year.

# Carol of the Birds

Birds have no direct relation to Christmas. The biblical story of the Nativity does not mention them, and the traditional accouterments which have accumulated around the holiday over the centuries do not especially include them. Nevertheless, there have been many carols which in some way allude to these winged inhabitants of the air, and no less than six Christmas songs have the title "Carol of the Birds."

There is the 1943 American carol by John Jacobs Niles (1892-1980) and the twentieth-century Australian piece by John Wheeler and William Garnet James (1895- ). From Czechoslovakia comes the modern folk song "Zezulka z lesa vylítla" or in English, "Carol of the Birds," "The Birds," or "From out the Forest a Cuckoo Flew." From southern France come "Le Noël des oiseaux" and "Noël des ausels," two folk carols from the sixteenth century or somewhat after. Both translate as "Carol of the Birds" with the latter song also known as "Whence Comes This Rush of Wings Afar." From Catalonia in Spain comes the possibly medieval composition, "El cant dels ocells" or, again, "Carol of the Birds." The international fascination with Christmas birds is most intriguing. Perhaps the motivation for such an emphasis is the beauty and positiveness which is common to both the lively, living creatures and the lively, living holiday.

# The Chipmunk Song

For the first 39 years of his life, Ross Bagdasarian (1919-1972) was perhaps best known as an actor in Hollywood movies. From 1952 to 1958 he appeared in supporting roles in nine feature films, including the screen classics *Stalag 17* (1953) and *Rear Window* (1954). Then in 1958 he created a gimmick Christmas song under the pseudonym David Seville. With the use of speeded-up tape recording, he was able to somewhat imitate the high-pitched, squeaky, and cute sounds of chipmunks. Although the song (also called "Christmas, Don't Be Late") really does not have especially good words or melody, the novelty effect of Alvin, Theodore, and Simon singing a "trio" in harmony was extremely popular for several years. The novelty has not completely worn off, for the tiny and tinny tones of the chipmunks have become a fixture of the Christmas season in the United States.

Because of this inventive little piece, Bagdasarian, who could not write music, won fame and fortune, receiving a Grammy Award from the Academy of Arts and Sciences for the best children's recording of 1958. It is the only song for which he is particularly remembered, although he did produce other compositions, including the popular novelty songs "Come On-a My House" (1950), with his Pulitzer Prize-winning cousin, William Saroyan, and "The Witch Doctor" (1958). Yet there is another significant legacy from Bagdasarian. In the 1980s a long-running television cartoon show was developed, based on the characters created in his 1958 song. (This program actually was an updated version of a short-lived series in 1961-1962.) For quite a few years after his untimely death by natural causes, therefore, David Seville and the three chipmunks continued to live on, not just in the Christmas season, but all year round.

# The Christmas Nightingale

The nightingale is a small bird of the thrush family that is especially noted for its fine nocturnal melodies. The loveliness of its song has inspired several musical works including a 1914 opera and a 1920 ballet by Igor Stravinsky (1882-1971), and a German folk carol, "Lieb Nachtigall, Wach Auf!" One of the better "bird carols," "Lieb Nachtigall" or "Die Weihnachtsnachtigall" is probably a product of seventeenth-century Franconia, in southwestern Germany. Its most common English translation is "The Christmas Nightingale," but the titles "Dear Nightingale, Awake" and "Wake, Nightingale" have also been used. Excluding the very famous carol "The Twelve Days of Christmas," which has birds all over the song including the pear-tree partridge, the contest for finest phenomenon featuring feathered fauna is between "The Christmas Nightingale," the southern French folk carol "Noël des ausels" ("Whence Comes This Rush of Wings Afar"), and the Czech folk carol "Zezulka z lesa vylítla" ("From out the Forest a Cuckoo Flew"). The nightingale may well fly home with the honors, though, due to its attractive and cheery music complemented by the particular delicacy and sweetness of its animal image.

# Do You Hear What I Hear?

In Christian religious tradition the lamb is a symbol of particular significance. The Old Testament Hebrews made sacrifices with lambs, and in the New Testament the Lamb of God is a synonym for Christ. Possibly this body of symbolism was consciously or unconsciously in the minds of the authors of the excellent 1962 carol, "Do You Hear What I Hear?" when they created the opening line, "Said the Night Wind to the Little Lamb." But whether or not this was the intent of Noel Regney and Gloria Shayne, it has been the effect.

For although "Do You Hear What I Hear?" is one of the better-known American popular Christmas songs of recent decades, to describe it simply as a popular carol would be quite misleading. It is also to a large extent a song with both religious content and religious style. That is, it approaches the nature of a hymn even though it may never achieve that status. The smooth, devout, and calm lyricism of the melody and the sensitive, indirect references to the Christmas story combine to create an atmosphere which is different from most other holiday songs of its era. It is the only well-known American Christmas song since World War II with a clearly religious tone.

"The Little Drummer Boy," which has become popular since 1945, has some suggestions of religious purpose but does not really qualify as a postwar song since it was first published in 1941. The 15 carols of Alfred Burt published in 1954 deal overall with the sacred aspects of Christmas but are far from being in the forefront of the American celebration of Christmas. "Do You Hear What I Hear?" therefore qualifies as the sole significant recent American representative to the body of religious Christmas carols. Unfortunately it is also the sole musical piece by either Regney or Shayne that has caught the imagination of a sizable segment of the American public.

# The Friendly Beasts

As a whole, there is a direct correlation between historical age and historical certainty. So it is expected that a twelfth-century tune might be imperfectly understood as to its origins. In contrast, it is not expected that a twentieth-century lyric be almost completely obscure as to its creation. Yet these are exactly the circumstances in the strange saga of "The Friendly Beasts."

In fact, just as much is known about the medieval tune as is known about the almost contemporary words. The simple and pleasant anonymous melody was used for the Latin hymn "Orientis Partibus," which reportedly was a part of the Donkey's Festival of the twelfth century. The music probably came from France, although England is also a possible place of origin. The imaginative lyrics, which present a fanciful conversation between several animals at the time of Jesus' birth, were probably written by a Robert Davis, and probably in the United States. The earliest known text was printed in 1934, but it may well be older. Copyright on the words did not occur until 1949. Davis is totally obscure, and combining the biographical emptiness with the considerable chronological uncertainty has resulted in a marked historical vacuum. It is unfortunate that Davis has not been clearly identified, for he deserves more recognition for the unusual medieval/modern carol to which he has given birth. There have been a number of other carols which depict the presenting of gifts to the Christ child, but none in which a donkey, cow, sheep, and dove have been the donors.

# Rudolph the Red-Nosed Reindeer

Reindeer are not a recent topic for Christmas songs. Ever since Clement Moore developed the modern myth of Santa Claus in his 1822 classic "'Twas the Night Before Christmas," reindeer have been closely associated with Santa and have been mentioned in carols. As far back as the 1850s or 1860s, Benjamin Hanby alluded to the animals in his "Up on the Housetop." Two other holiday songs with reindeer featured were Ken Darby's 1942 musical rendition of Moore's poem and the 1946 hit, "Here Comes Santa Claus" by Gene Autry and Oakley Haldeman.

But Johnny Marks' 1949 phenomenon "Rudolph the Red-Nosed Reindeer" was a lot more than the mere mention of deer. Rudolph was the first important new Christmas character since Moore's introduction of the magnanimous Christmas elf. The success of Rudolph apparently encouraged the subsequent appearance of other imaginative and lasting fictional personalities such as Frosty the Snowman, the Chipmunks, and the Grinch. In addition, Marks' song, although not the first highly popular novelty carol to appear after World War II, was the supreme prototype of Christmas novelties and possibly served as the impetus for similar songs later on.

Marks, though, was not the creator of the Rudolph character. In 1939, Marks' brother-in-law, Robert L. May, developed the story of Rudolph as part of an advertising promotion for Montgomery Ward stores. In 1947, Ward's graciously gave the copyright for Rudolph to May, who published the tale in book form that year. Instantly the little volume became a best-seller. No doubt inspired by the extraordinary success of May's book, Marks adapted the delightful story into equally charming lyrics, added a very catchy tune, obtained a big-name recording artist, and an even more extraordinary commercial success soon ensued. The initial recorder of "Rudolph," movie cowboy and country-western singer Gene Autry, was not new to the Christmas record game or to the reindeer game. Somewhat earlier

he had sung his own composition "Here Comes Santa Claus" into
the hearts of holiday audiences. "Rudolph," however, far surpassed
the popularity of Autry's previous recording, quickly reaching the
top of the pop music ratings near the end of 1949. It made Marks
(1909-1985) an overnight celebrity and facilitated his later composition of a batch of other holiday songs.

Only one other twentieth-century American popular carol, "White
Christmas," has exceeded the public acceptance of "Rudolph." Recorded in many versions, selling many millions of records, "Rudolph" has rapidly evolved into a singular Christmas institution. A
variety of holiday merchandise has been marketed based on the
beloved little animal whose brightly shining nose led Santa and his
sleigh through the crisis of a foggy Christmas Eve. And not one, but
three holiday specials were produced with Rudolph as the star. In
1964 the annual favorite *Rudolph the Red-Nosed Reindeer*, with
"Snowman" Burl Ives narrating and singing, was first telecast. Two
follow-up programs, *Rudolph's Shiny New Year* (1976), narrated by
Red Skelton, and *Rudolph and Frosty*, were unfortunately not nearly
as well received. All of these supplemental activities, though, have
helped to keep Rudolph and his nose and the forefront of the ongoing
secular celebration of Christmas.

# NOVELTY SONGS

# All I Want for Christmas
# Is My Two Front Teeth

One of the more unusual experiences of twentieth-century American culture was the music (or whatever you call it) of Spike Jones and his City Slickers. Jones (1911-1965), whose real name was Lindley A. Jones, irreverently inflicted on delighted American audiences his uninhibited comedy antics under the guise of musical performance. Among his most memorable contributions was the crude and brash anti-Hitler song "Der Fuehrer's Face," which gave comedic relief to World War II. Soon after the war he helped to popularize the novelty song "All I Want for Christmas Is My Two Front Teeth" by producing a best-selling recording in 1948.

The song actually was written in 1946. Its author was Donald Yetter Gardner (1913- ), a composer, conductor, and music educator who was born in Pennsylvania. "All I Want" was his only well-known song. The elements of novelty which made it very popular in the late 1940s, and moderately so in the present time, were the almost complete absence of Christmas references, the child's wish to recover his teeth as a Christmas gift, and the cute effect of air passing through the faulty dentition. Gardner's song was the first of a long series of highly successful postwar novelty carols which focused on unconventional holiday ingredients.

# Frosty the Snowman

"Frosty the Snowman," which was written in 1950, was in several ways an imaginative echo of "Rudolph the Red-Nosed Reindeer" which appeared the year before. Like Rudolph, Frosty was a magical new Christmas character who evoked both delight and sadness. Frosty brought much joy to the children who put the old silk hat on his head, thus bringing him to life. There also were some tears shed when Frosty began to melt away and had to leave. But his promise to return ended the tale with the anticipation of renewed friendship. Like Rudolph, his appearance was expected to be annual.

The perennial nature of Frosty has greatly aided his public acceptance and commercial success. The clever story by Walter E. ("Jack") Rollins (1906-1973) and the rather good melody by Steve Edward Nelson (1907- ) of course are the key building blocks of "Frosty"'s tremendous popularity. (New Yorkers Rollins and Nelson also developed another musical holiday character, "Peter Cottontail" (1949), which is the best-known recent Easter personality.)

Also like Rudolph, Frosty has been aggressively merchandised and has had three television specials to help sustain Frosty in the mind's eye of millions. In 1969, Jimmy Durante narrated an excellent cartoon version of Frosty's birth, life, and demise. Variant adventures of Frosty were presented in the 1979 program, *Frosty's Winter Wonderland*, presided over by Andy Griffith, and in *Rudolph and Frosty*. But all the borrowing between Rudolph and Frosty was not one-sided. When the most successful television program about Rudolph was put on the air in 1964, the jolly host of the show was none other than a snowman!

# The Little Drummer Boy

Two old themes converge in the charming modern carol "The Little Drummer Boy." Theme one is the centuries-old practice of presenting gifts to the Christ child. Theme two is the depiction of drums in Christmas carols. In the seventeenth- or eighteenth-century English folk classic "The Twelve Days of Christmas," the highest number is assigned to drummers drumming. And in the delightful French carol of about the same period, "Patapan," the drum is the main theme and a drum-like beat is the basis of the rhythm.

To these borrowed concepts were added the delightful tale of a little boy who travels to the manger and offers a unique present of love–his talent at drumming. This beloved carol was first published in 1941 under the title "Carol of the Drum." Its creator, Missourian Katherine K. Davis (1892-1980), was a highly respected composer of serious music including operettas, choral works, and hymn tunes. In 1958, the name of the song was changed to "The Little Drummer Boy," and Henry V. Onorati (1912- ) and Harry Simeone (1911- ) were subsequently listed as collaborators. The title change and its adjacent events apparently sparked a change in the fortunes of the carol from relative obscurity to considerable fame. Nine years after its "rebirth," extensive popular interest led to the production of a television special, *The Little Drummer Boy*, narrated by Greer Garson. A second production, *The Little Drummer Boy, Book Two*, again guided by the voice of Garson, was telecast in 1976. These two sequels to "The Little Drummer Boy" clearly demonstrate the affectionate place of this little carol in our contemporary American culture.

# Patapan

Burgundy is a color, a type of wine, and a historical region in eastern France which at one time was extremely powerful. Burgundy is also one of France's prime areas for the development of carols. Much of the carol activity in Burgundy came from the pen of Bernard de la Monnoye (1641-1728), the carol poet laureate of Burgundy. Several of his Christmas poems are still printed in the twentieth century, including the interestingly titled songs "Tantara! Mighty God!" and "Cheerily Wife! The Devil Is Dead!" as well as the bright under-known classic, "Patapan."

All of Monnoye's carols were probably written around 1700 and all are set to tunes which are probably from the folk resources of contemporary Burgundy but may have been composed by Monnoye himself. The cheerful and rhythmic "Patapan," which exhorts little Willie to get his little drum and tap-tap-tap on it, is a brisker and richer predecessor to "The Little Drummer Boy." The recent song, in contrast, does have the advantage of a sensitive and heart-warming narrative. Musically, though, "Patapan" is superior to "Drummer Boy" and the majority of other carols from any period.

# Suzy Snowflake

At first glance, the popular children's carol "Suzy Snowflake" may seem as fragile and flimsy as the character it portrays. But "Suzy" must be constructed of more substantial material than crystalline water, for that meteorological musical miniature has not melted away in spite of the passing of several decades. Conceived in 1951 by Sid Tepper (1918- ), from Manhattan, and Roy C. Bennett (1918- ), from Brooklyn, "Suzy" survives because of the warmth and simple charm of its lyrics and light melody.

Another Christmas song for which Tepper and Bennett jointly provided both words and music, the 1955 novelty "Nuttin' for Christmas," has some of the same traits though in smaller amounts. The two composers also collaborated on a number of other musical works, including the popular ballads "Red Roses for a Blue Lady" (1948) and "Naughty Lady of Shady Lane" (1954). Their most lovable song, however, might well be "Suzy Snowflake." So the next time you see a little particle of snow descending on a December day, think of it not as the beginning of a snowstorm but as a subtle announcement that Suzy's back in town.

# Toyland

Stan Laurel (1890-1965) and Oliver Hardy (1892-1957) have delighted several generations with their zany movie antics. They were at the height of their comedic capabilities when they made the 1934 film *Babes in Toyland*. The movie, of course, was an offshoot of the 1903 operetta of the same name by the great Irish-American stage composer Victor Herbert (1859-1924). The pièce de résistance of the very charming and melodic depiction of the fanciful "little girl and boy land" was the song "Toyland."

Providing the lyrics for Herbert's smooth and dreamy music was Brooklyn-born Glen MacDonough (1870-1924), who is known for little else. Technically, the words have no direct affiliation with the traditions of Christmas. But the spirit of the song, about the great pleasure that toys bring to children, is so very compatible with the loving and giving essence of the December holiday. Herbert and MacDonough, furthermore, have sensitively captured the fleeting moments of childhood in their musical magical realm, so that children of all ages, including the Laurel and Hardy characters, can occasionally return inside the borders of Toyland in spite of the warning with which the song ends.

# The Twelve Days of Christmas

Why are old MacDonald's farm and "The Twelve Days of Christmas" kindred entities? First, they both use accumulating devices in their well-known songs. Second, animals are common in both, with MacDonald having pigs, chickens, goats, cows, and so on, and "Twelve Days" having turtledoves, French hens, calling birds, geese, swans, and first but not least, the personable partridge. Third, both are lively, enduring, and highly popular folk novelty pieces.

With these three shared attributes, however, the similarities between the two fade away. While "MacDonald's" is an American phenomenon, "Twelve Days" is English, or even possibly French, in origin. Created in the seventeenth or eighteenth century, by best guess near their intersection, "Twelve Days" was first published around 1780. Although the lyrics are clearly from England, and the skillful and polished tune presumably also from there, a similar folk song is also known in France. This suggests that the imaginative and well-executed concepts in "Twelve Days" may have been borrowed from across the English Channel.

"Twelve Days" is such a versatile and plastic song that it has the tendency to attract tinkering, substitutions, and variations. There have been several versions of the lyrics, including at least one created in the United States. Its centuries-old counting feature, which is common in nursery rhymes, is a favorite toy for musical amusement. What separates "Twelve Days" from other counting songs are the relative sophistication and clever imagery of the lyrics, the accessible and high-quality melody, and the attachment of the words and music to the most appreciated of our annual occasions. The pleasant notion of possibly receiving the unusual array of gifts enumerated in "Twelve Days," in addition, is surely another point of considerable endearment.

# Welcome Christmas

Many Americans as well as others have heard the song "Welcome Christmas," yet relatively few could unequivocally state that they have done so. The song, furthermore, is seldom in carol collections or in recorded anthologies, yet it can be heard every Christmas season. What is this musical will-o'-the-wisp? It is the wisp of a song which begins "Fah who foraze" and which is sung every December by the Whos in Who-ville. Yes, "Welcome Christmas" is the pleasant little ditty which espouses the spirit of Christmas in the television holiday classic, *How the Grinch Stole Christmas*.

The animated cartoon special with the resonant voice of Boris Karloff and the delightful tale by the highly talented and immensely popular children's author, Dr. Seuss (Theodor Seuss Geisel [1904-1991]), first aired in 1966. Arguably, it is the best holiday program for children of all ages ever broadcast in the United States. "Welcome Christmas" is the highlight of the production and although it cannot be classified as a great song, its warmth and suitability as well as its context make it, in its peculiar way, an American music holiday legend.

In addition to the cute lyrics by Seuss and the smooth music by Albert Hague (1920- ), much of the charm of this carol is its concept of directly greeting the holiday with a song as contrasted with the usual custom of celebrating the holiday in song. This joyous confrontation of Christmas is not new or unique, for as far back as the fifteenth century, an English folk song met the holiday in a similar fashion with the lyrics "Welcome Yule, Thou Merry Man." A closely related poem, "Wolcum Yole!," was possibly concocted in the sixteenth century, and the continuum reaches into the twentieth century when the English master Benjamin Britten (1913-1976) composed an excellent setting for "Wolcum Yole!" as part of his 1942 *A Ceremony of Carols*. At least some things, it appears, stay the same.

# HOLIDAY MEMORIES

# The Christmas Song

To call any song "The Christmas Song" as if there were no others may seem to be a bit arrogant. But in line with the old saying "If it's true, it isn't bragging," the 1946 ballad fits quite well with the title chosen for it. The smooth, sentimental, even beautiful carol by Mel Tormé (1925- ) and Robert Wells is as fine an impression of the positive nature, friendliness, and spirituality of Christmas ever managed by an entirely secular song. Not only is it an ideal vehicle for preserving the pleasant memories of Christmas, it has a quality uncommon among popular songs, that is, a sense of depth.

This Tin Pan Alley masterpiece, also known under its more neutral first line, "Chestnuts Roasting on an Open Fire," came toward the beginning of its authors' very successful careers. (It was written, incidentally, as well as recorded by Nat King Cole, in the middle of a summer heat wave when humans were being roasted by the open fire of the sun.) Nicknamed "The Velvet Fog," Tormé, from Chicago, was a nightclub, radio, and television singer as well as a composer. He also had an ongoing, indirect minor role in the 1980s television comedy series *Night Court*. He was the favorite singer of the main character, the unconventional young judge. Tormé actually appeared on the show several times. Wells (actually Robert Wells Levinson), from Washington State, was a multifaceted artist. He was the creator of a large variety of songs and movie scores and wrote and produced nightclub acts and television specials for a number of top performers. Included in his achievements were six Emmys and the Writers Guild Annual Award. However, nothing else done by Tormé or Wells is as appreciated or esthetic as their joint holiday composition which continues to live up to its most audacious name.

# Home for the Holidays

It could not have been phrased any better. "Oh, there's no place like home for the holidays" is a perfect expression of the feelings of most persons when December inevitably appears on the calendar. And when the mutually shared thoughts penned by Al Stillman (1906-1979) were enhanced by the moving melody created by Robert Allen (1927- ), it should be no surprise that the 1954 composition became one of the happy standards of Christmastime. Also helping the acceptance of the song was its perfect timing. It appeared during a period of peace, prosperity, and stability in the United States, a year after the end of the Korean War and almost a decade after World War II.

New Yorker Stillman and Allen, of Troy, New York, also combined their talents on some other songs including the very good romantic ballads "Chances Are" (1957), "It's Not for Me to Say" (1956), and "No, Not Much" (1956). In these songs the authors were able to distill for common consumption some of the more difficult to express emotional experiences of people in love. In contrast, the sentiments in "Home for the Holidays" are neither novel nor rarely verbalized. What Stillman and Allen did was to fully appreciate the almost universal reverie of spending Christmas wherever we call home, and to very capably convert the dreams and hopes into a readily absorbed musical reality.

# I'll Be Home for Christmas

Nostalgic songs about home, family, and sweethearts are normal in the times of war. The "Big War," World War II, had its share of such emotion-touching compositions. One of the best of that period, written at the midpoint of the American participation in the conflict, was the 1943 carol, "I'll Be Home for Christmas." Its first line, "I'm dreaming tonight of a place I love," is very indicative of the sentiments of this excellent ballad.

"I'll Be Home" is the second most remembered work of poet James Kimball ("Kim") Gannon (1900-1974), from Brooklyn, and musician Walter Kent (1911- ), from Manhattan. Kent also wrote the music for the 1941 classic "The White Cliffs of Dover," to accompany the lyrics by Nat Burton. It was also among the most unforgettable recordings featuring the baritone smoothness of Bing Crosby. Due to its very personal yet widely appealing lyrics, and its appropriately tender yet confidently transporting melody, it has lasted many years beyond the distressing war period of separation. Long after the reunions with friends and relatives were over, and the uniforms hung in the back closets, the song has continued to serve as a medium for past holiday reminiscences, and for future nostalgia.

# White Christmas

Because "White Christmas" may be the most popular American secular Christmas carol, rivaled only by "Jingle Bells," it could easily be presumed that it was treated as a star from the moment of its 1940 conception by the incomparable song writer Irving Berlin (1888-1989). Before its first presentation to the public, though, in the 1942 black-and-white movie *Holiday Inn*, the expected hit of Berlin's score was to be the Valentine's Day song, "Be Careful, It's My Heart." That song quickly lost out to "White Christmas" and has more or less been relegated to the status of a historical footnote in comparison to its highly celebrated score mate.

The honors for "White Christmas" commenced soon after its premiere. It received the Oscar for best song of 1942. It was recorded by Bing Crosby, who had sung it in *Holiday Inn*, and that version eventually became the single best-selling record of all time. It precipitated the remake of *Holiday Inn* in 1954, the second version being in color and having the only possible title, *White Christmas*. In the 1942 movie Crosby was one of the stars along with Fred Astaire and Marjorie Reynolds. In the 1954 movie Crosby was undoubtedly the leading attraction (after the song, of course), in spite of the star-filled supporting cast of Danny Kaye, Vera-Ellen, and Rosemary Clooney. The later movie, a more glossy and sentimental production, was in several ways even better than the earlier one.

"White Christmas," with its nostalgic and unspecific lyrics about the pleasures of Christmases past and its softly floating music which glides without impediment across the mental pictures of tree tops, sleigh bells, snow, and Christmas cards, is perhaps the finest twentieth-century carol from any country. It is the highlight of Bing Crosby's singularly successful career, and the leading light of Irving Berlin's immense output of popular songs save for the patriotic masterpiece, "God Bless America." Just as "God Bless America" is widely designated as the unofficial second national anthem of the United States, "White Christmas" could be decorated with a similar laurel, that of official national popular song.

\* \* \*

May your days be merry and bright,
And I hope this Christmas reader was just right.

# Title Index

# Person and Group Index

*217*